BARRON'S BOOK NOTES

SOPHOCLES'

Oedipus Trilogy

BY

Gerald Lee Ratliff
Associate Professor
Montclair State College

SERIES EDITOR

Michael Spring
Editor, *Literary Cavalcade*
Scholastic Inc.

W9-BZE-679

BARRON'S

BARRON'S EDUCATIONAL SERIES, INC.
Woodbury, New York / London / Toronto / Sydney

ACKNOWLEDGMENTS

We would like to acknowledge the many painstaking hours of work Holly Hughes and Thomas F. Hirsch have devoted to making the *Book Notes* series a success.

All inquiries should be addressed to:
Barron's Educational Series, Inc.
113 Crossways Park Drive
Woodbury, New York 11797

Library of Congress Catalog Card No. 84-18532

International Standard Book No. 0-8120-3430-9

Library of Congress Cataloging in Publication Data
Ratliff, Gerald Lee.
  Sophocles' Oedipus trilogy.

  (Barron's book notes)
  Bibliography: p. 102
  Summary: A guide to reading the Oedipus trilogy
with a critical and appreciative mind. Includes
background on the author's life and times, sample
tests, term paper suggestions, and a reading list.
    1. Sophocles. Oedipus Rex. 2. Sophocles.
Oedipus at Colonus. 3. Sophocles. Antigone.
4. Oedipus (Greek mythology) in literature.
5. Antigone (Legendary character) in literature.
[1. Sophocles. Oedipus Rex. 2. Sophocles. Oedipus
at Colonus. 3. Sophocles. Antigone. 4. Classical
literature—History and criticism] I. Title.
II. Series.
PA4417.R37 1984   882'.01   84-18532
ISBN 0-8120-3430-9 (pbk.)

CONTENTS

ADVISORY BOARD

HOW TO USE THIS BOOK

You have to know how to approach literature in order to get the most out of it. This *Barron's Book Notes* volume follows a plan based on methods used by some of the best students to read a work of literature.

Begin with the guide's section on the author's life and times. As you read, try to form a clear picture of the author's personality, circumstances, and motives for writing the work. This background usually will make it easier for you to hear the author's tone of voice, and follow where the author is heading.

Then go over the rest of the introductory material—such sections as those on the plot, characters, setting, themes, and style of the work. Underline, or write down in your notebook, particular things to watch for, such as contrasts between characters and repeated literary devices. At this point, you may want to develop a system of symbols to use in marking your text as you read. (Of course, you should only mark up a book you own, not one that belongs to another person or a school.) Perhaps you will want to use a different letter for each character's name, a different number for each major theme of the book, a different color for each important symbol or literary device. Be prepared to mark up the pages of your book as you read. Put your marks in the margins so you can find them again easily.

Now comes the moment you've been waiting for—the time to start reading the work of literature. You may want to put aside your *Barron's Book Notes* volume until you've read the work all the way through. Or you may want to alternate, reading the *Book Notes* analysis of each section as soon as you have finished reading the corresponding part of the original. Before you move on, reread crucial passages you don't fully understand. (Don't take this guide's analysis for granted—make up your own mind as to what the work means.)

Once you've finished the whole work of literature, you may want to review it right away, so you can firm up your ideas about what it means. You may want to leaf through the book concentrating on passages you marked in reference to one character or one theme. This is also a good time to reread the *Book Notes* introductory material, which pulls together insights on specific topics.

When it comes time to prepare for a test or to write a paper, you'll already have formed ideas about the work. You'll be able to go back through it, refreshing your memory as to the author's exact words and perspective, so that you can support your opinions with evidence drawn straight from the work. Patterns will emerge, and ideas will fall into place; your essay question or term paper will almost write itself. Give yourself a dry run with one of the sample tests in the guide. These tests present both multiple-choice and essay questions. An accompanying section gives answers to the multiple-choice questions as well as suggestions for writing the essays. If you have to select a term paper topic, you may choose one from the list of suggestions in this book. This guide also provides you with a reading list, to help you when you start research for a term paper, and a selection of provocative comments by critics, to spark your thinking before you write.

THE AUTHOR AND HIS TIMES

The Athens that Sophocles knew in the fifth century B.C. was a curious place. By modern standards it was a small and uncomfortable city. There was no running water, no central heating, and no adequate transportation. The average Athenian was poorly paid, uneducated, and probably would rather watch athletic contests than go to the theater.

Yet, amazingly, fifth-century Athens became a fountainhead of Western civilization in the study of history, architecture, sculpture, philosophy, and drama. No one can really explain why all this happened in that city at that time—unless it was because the Athenians' enormous spirit and energy led them to explore their world with a keen eye and an open mind. Like the early American settlers, the Athenians were a proud, independent, and fierce people who resisted any attempts to enslave them. Having fought off invasions by the Persian Empire from the east, and by others from the south, they were fired with a sense of patriotism and self-confidence. They knew their city was the dominant city in Greece.

Athens was an autonomous city-state, or *polis*, like most of the cities in ancient Greece. It had adopted a form of government that helped it survive the chaotic times of foreign invasions—a kind of democracy that encouraged open assembly of all nonslave male citizens, and gave equal rights to them, much as today's New England town meetings do. Local officials were elected to office and served until they were defeated in another election by another opponent. Sophocles himself was twice elected to a government position and served with distinction in the armed forces. This democracy, however, wasn't quite as enlightened as it sounds. Women and slaves weren't allowed any voice in government. Sophocles was a member of the ruling class, but he could see that the system wasn't perfect.

The small population and the town-meeting form of government encouraged Athenian citizens to participate actively in public affairs, and to try to decide their own political and social destinies. They were required by law to present their own defenses before a jury of their peers if they were taken to court. Public law also required that Athenians compete in athletics, which was considered part of their physical and moral obligation to the nation. (From this, of course, the Olympic Games were born.) The Athenian of Sophocles' time was thus forced by law to act personally in situations that today we automatically leave to the experts. It was difficult for citizens to avoid participating in this system. You could protest about things you saw that were wrong—as Sophocles certainly did— but you were expected to keep up your civic responsibilities, too. This culture focused on the dignity of the individual and his power over his own fate.

These were the times in which Sophocles lived and wrote his plays. Born in the early years of the fifth century B.C., Sophocles was witness to an era of military exploration, political turmoil, and social revolution—all of which he included in his plays. As the youngest son of a wealthy merchant, Sophocles was well educated and was accustomed to luxuries that the average Athenian couldn't afford. His wealth and education, however, didn't prevent him from becoming a sensitive and fair observer of Athenian life. In his lifetime Sophocles served Athens as a soldier, a politician, and finally a wise, old counselor. But his greatest contribution was as a writer.

Frequently called the "greatest" of Greek tragic playwrights, Sophocles wrote more than one hundred plays. The seven that survive are *Ajax* (written c. 445 B.C.), *Antigone* (c. 442), *Oedipus the King* (c. 425), *Philoctetes* (c. 409), *Electra* and *Trachiniae* (c. 408), and *Oedipus at Colonus* (c. 407). All of these plays reflect what Sophocles saw and felt during his lifetime, and they were bold, serious statements. When you read these plays you will discover that Sophocles predicted the impending decline of Athens, pointing to the city's moral decay and religious hypocrisy. He also foretold the injustice and prejudice that would arise if the Athenian democracy didn't protect the rights of minorities. He was ashamed of the cruel treatment of war slaves and was saddened by the poverty of the peasants and hired workers. Like a modern-day Abraham Lincoln, Sophocles issued an "Athenian Address" in his plays and warned the audience of impending doom if they didn't change their ways.

Many such predictions are found in the Oedipus trilogy, and as you read the characters' dialogue and observe their actions, keep in mind that the plays were meant to stand as grim warnings. Most of Sophocles' audience couldn't read or write, but Sophocles felt that if they *heard* his message they might be saved from destruction. Therefore, he dramatized legends the audience would already know. He organized his plays in simple episodes and included songs to give the play a rhythm that was easy to follow. This, he felt, would help the average person receive moral instruction just by viewing the play. If Sophocles had lived today, he would probably have understood exactly how to use television to sway people to his political views.

Why did a leading citizen like Sophocles start writing plays to get his message across? It's important to realize that theater was not considered entertainment in Athens. Drama was a regular part of the religious life of the city. Each theatrical performance was thought of as an act of worship, honoring the god Dionysus. Dramatic festivals dedicated to Dionysus were held in late March and throughout the first week of April. Theater was allowed only during this festival time, so it was an event that brought the community together. We have similar town festivals today to celebrate holidays, like Labor Day and the Fourth of July.

The weeks set aside to honor Dionysus were so sacred that all shops and offices were closed. Some jails even freed their prisoners. The spectacular state-sponsored celebration brought in visitors and VIPs from all parts of the world, like a world premiere of a film might do today. At first, admission to the festival was free. Later, when admission was by donation, a public fund was established to enable those who couldn't otherwise afford it to attend.

All Athenians were expected to attend the festival, held at the Theatre of Dionysus on the slope of the Acropolis. The audience, as you might expect, was not a select group. The theater had a capacity of about 14,000. The audience included old men, soldiers, farmers, sailors, teachers, athletes, carpenters, and students. They sat on marble benches in the open air, surrounding the stage on three sides. They were a lively audience, likely to burst into tears if they were moved (they were just as likely to boo or hiss if they didn't like the play). Yet they were expected to conduct themselves respectfully. Severe penalties and fines were levied for lewd behavior, and the records show that occasionally spectators were forcefully removed from the theater.

For the most part, however, the festival was a dignified and solemn affair. The audience assembled at sunrise and sat through three tragedies, a short farcical play, and a comedy all in one day. At the end of the festival prizes were awarded by a jury of spectators, local politicians, and dignitaries appointed by lot. First prize was a crown of ivy (Sophocles was reported to have won twenty-two such prizes). The playwright wasn't interested in making money from the play, nor was the producer. Usually the producer was a wealthy citizen who donated money to stage the play as a token of his public service. Again, private individuals—amateurs, so to speak—performed the jobs we think only trained professionals can do, and they did it not for profit but for the good of the state, as a public duty.

The spectators viewed the play as a vital moral lesson, and they came expecting to hear life's most serious problems discussed. They had no other forms of dramatic entertainment—no television or movies. For them, watching other people acting out a story—even a familiar legend, such as the legend of Oedipus—would have been a very special occasion.

As you read the play, try to visualize the historical times and the theatrical traditions that have been described here. Then try to imagine yourself as a fifth-century Athenian sitting in an open-aired amphitheater watching Oedipus advance toward his tragic end. Perhaps you will forget your own problems and identify with those of Oedipus. When you are able to do that, you will have captured the spirit of the times and the spirit of the play.

THE OEDIPUS TRILOGY

The Legend of Oedipus

The classical legend of Oedipus first appears in Greek literature as early as the writings of Homer (700 B.C.), author of the *Iliad* and the *Odyssey*. It would have also been well known to the Athenians of Sophocles' time from popular poems and short stories of the period. Fix the legend in your mind before you look at the way Sophocles presented it.

It was prophesied that Laios and Iocaste, king and queen of Thebes, would give birth to a child who would grow up to murder his father and marry his mother. Fearing this dreadful prophecy, the parents nailed their first son's feet together—hence the name Oedipus, which means "swollen-foot"—and left him to die on a lonely mountainside outside the city. However, he was found by a wandering shepherd who took the baby to the nearby city of Corinth. There he was adopted by the childless King Polybos and Queen Merope, who raised him as a prince in the royal household. He never knew they weren't his real parents.

When he was a young adult, Oedipus first heard the prophecy. Assuming that this applied to Polybos and Merope, the only parents Oedipus had ever known, he fled Corinth and wandered around Greece. During his wandering he met a group of travelers and killed an old man who, unknown to him, was his *real* father, King Laios. Later Oedipus arrived at Thebes and met the Sphinx, a monster who guarded the gates of the city. When Oedipus correctly answered the riddle asked by the Sphinx, he was rewarded with the title of king of Thebes and was given the hand of the recently widowed queen, Iocaste. Needless to say, no one knew that she was his real mother. They had four children—Antigone, Ismene, Eteocles, and Polyneices.

As the king of Thebes, Oedipus ruled in wealth and prosperity for some time. Soon, however, a mysterious plague swept the city. The sacred oracles foretold that the plague could be removed only by the discovery of Laios' murderer. Oedipus sends Creon, his brother-in-law, to Delphi to consult the oracles and find out the identity of the murderer. This is how Oedipus discovers his own identity and that of his parents, and discovers his sins. In his despair, he blinds himself, and Iocaste hangs herself. Oedipus is exiled, and Creon takes over the throne of Thebes.

Oedipus wanders through Greece for twenty years, accompanied by his daughter Antigone. Finally he finds himself outside Colonus, where he asks for sanctuary. He is tired and he wants someplace to die in peace. Theseus, king of Athens, grants Oedipus sanctuary there.

Meanwhile, there has been another prophecy: Whatever city has the grave of Oedipus will be assured of eternal prosperity. Creon hears the prophecy and tries to get Oedipus to return to Thebes—he even tries force—but Oedipus refuses and dies at Colonus.

There has been a power struggle going on back at Thebes. Oedipus and Iocaste's two sons, Eteocles and Polyneices, have been named corulers of Thebes, but each wants the throne for himself. Polyneices assembles an army and attacks the city. Eteocles, aided by

Creon, tries to resist the onslaught. At the end of this bloody battle for power Eteocles and Polyneices both lie dead, and Creon regains his throne.

Creon decrees that Eteocles, defender of Thebes, is entitled to a state funeral, but Polyneices, who attacked his own city, may have no funeral rites whatsoever. This was a grave and shocking punishment, which would prevent Polyneices' spirit from entering the afterworld.

Antigone is a loyal sister to Eteocles and Polyneices. In defiance of Creon's edict she buries Polyneices. As punishment, Creon condemns her to death. No more is heard of Ismene, and so ends the House of Oedipus.

The Characters

Sophocles doesn't mention his characters' ages or describe their appearances, so you need to imagine what they look and sound like. Only occasional hints in the dialogue and action describe character traits or mannerisms. Think of a tone of voice that might fit their lines of dialogue. Visualize them moving around on stage. Think of an appropriate costume that might suggest their character. If it helps, visualize modern people—actors you've seen or people you know—who could play these characters the way you think they should be played.

Oedipus

Try to visualize Oedipus as a forceful, powerful ruler who begins the trilogy in absolute control of the situation. As the story progresses, however, Oedipus' power and pride are broken down. How do you see him at the end of *Oedipus the King*? Some readers imagine a broken, pitiful old man who's been crushed by the avenging gods. Others see him as a wiser, soberer man, rising majestically above his misfortunes. How do you see him just before his death at the end of *Oedipus at Colonus*?

Although Oedipus is the title character of the first two plays, you don't know his exact age or his physical traits. Some readers believe that Sophocles left out these essential character details because he was more concerned with developing Oedipus' inner nature—his moral and ethical qualities—than in developing a character for performance by an actor. Other readers point out that the lack of details is characteristic of Sophocles' economical writing style. (Athenians would probably have already had a mental picture of the legendary Oedipus, anyway.)

Oedipus isn't given a lot of physical action, either. He enters, exits, kneels, prays, shouts, struts, weeps, yells, and dies. His most significant action is blinding himself, but that takes place offstage. Why does Sophocles omit physical movement for Oedipus? Perhaps Oedipus must seem stately and regal, so he will stand as a symbol of Thebes' political order, or as a symbol of political authority in general. Perhaps his restrained, grand actions emphasize his heroic, almost superhuman qualities. Consider these possible meanings when Oedipus first appears. Then, as the trilogy progresses, notice how he changes. As Oedipus loses his noble posture, he gradually becomes more like any other human.

From the information given in the script, you can sketch the following portrait of Oedipus. He is apparently handsome and well built. He is described as a "tower of strength," and has a penetrating way of looking at people. He is quick-tempered, and often acts impulsively and violently. His followers love him, and consider him a brilliant ruler because he solved the riddle of the Sphinx and brought prosperity to the city of Thebes.

When *Oedipus the King* begins, Oedipus exhibits wisdom, love for his children and his subjects, and a reputation for high moral standards. He has a passion for truth, and shows courage in the face of disaster or conflict. These same noble qualities, however, also lead to his inevitable tragic downfall. His wisdom becomes self-righteousness, and he refuses to believe anyone who doesn't agree with him. His love for his children becomes obsessive, and he refuses to see that he's married his own mother. His passion for the truth and high moral standards lead him in a fatal quest for the murderer of Laios.

The one trait of Oedipus that doesn't change in the course of the plays is his strength and courage in the face of disaster. As the net of guilt tightens on him with each revelation about the truth of the prophecy, Oedipus remains strong and resolved. Every step he takes to solve the mystery of Laios' murder brings him closer to self-exposure, yet he never hesitates to pursue that truth. When the last piece of the puzzle falls into place, Oedipus the detective has become Oedipus the criminal. But his courage and strength help him endure the pain and suffering that come with knowledge of what he has done.

Oedipus' search for the truth leads him to the discovery that he isn't a "child of luck," but a "man of misfortune." His fate was determined years before his birth, as proven by the prophecy of the oracles. All he can do is live out his destiny, but he does this with such dignity and heroism that he shows there is nobility even in suffering and despair. At the end of *Oedi-*

pus at Colonus you may respect Oedipus for pursuing the truth to its horrible conclusion. Having blinded himself, Oedipus is a broken and shaken man. But he also becomes a model for you to imitate. He has shown what it means to endure in the face of certain defeat. He has shown what it takes to survive in a world that is ruled by unpredictable fate. He has shown the true meaning of suffering and despair. He earns your respect and sympathy when he chooses to live rather than die, and to make his life an example to others of how guilt and pride may lead to self-knowledge. When you think of Oedipus, remember that he suffers for all of us, so that all of us can know the truth about ourselves in a world that will always be hostile and cruel.

Teiresias (Tiresias)

Teiresias is a wise, old man who has supernatural powers to interpret the past and predict the future. Think of him being like a modern psychic, gifted in the art of foretelling things to come. The fact that Teiresias is blind makes his visionary abilities even more mysterious. This may also lead Oedipus to deny Teiresias' ability to "see" the truth. He rarely volunteers information unless asked to do so, and speaks in a soft, whispering tone. At first Teiresias refuses to answer Oedipus' questions about the prophecy. He consents to reveal what the oracles have foretold about Oedipus' future only when he is threatened with death.

It was thought in Greek legends that Teiresias became a holy man when he was chosen by the gods to interpret their signs and symbols for all to understand. He appears as a character in many of the classical plays, and is always a spokesman for the gods. Therefore, when Oedipus insults Teiresias in the first scene of *Oedipus the King*, and accuses him of being a false prophet, he is also attacking the gods and is in danger of blasphemy. Oedipus is sealing his own doom when he dares to insult the holy man, and the Chorus is quick to point that out to him.

Although his appearance in the plays is brief, Teiresias sets the tone of the moral and religious beliefs of the gods. As their spokesman, Teiresias speaks in riddles and slogans. His sometimes puzzling predictions are intended to make men think about themselves and their actions. He does this extremely well in the first meeting with Oedipus, asking him to consider himself the murderer of Laios.

Teiresias acts as "ideal spectator." He observes the scene and comments when characters need guidance or direction. Teiresias can look into the hearts and souls of people, like he does when he defends Creon's innocence at the beginning of *Oedipus the King*.

Creon

Creon is Oedipus' brother-in-law and a trusted adviser to the king. He is also third-in-command of Thebes as a political leader. The Chorus mentions that he is an honest man who is reliable, trustworthy, and sensible. The Chorus also defends Creon against Oedipus' charge of conspiracy.

When you first meet Creon he has just returned from the oracles at Delphi. He is honorable and conscientious in his duty to Oedipus and to Thebes. He can't understand why Oedipus accuses him of conspiring with Teiresias to seize power. But honor is important to him—he is quick to defend his reputation and protest his innocence. He even suggests to the audience that he be put to death if Oedipus questions his loyalty.

You should feel alarm and outrage when Creon is exiled from Thebes. He is an innocent man whose common sense and sense of fair play could have been valuable to Oedipus. When he returns to Thebes at the end of *Oedipus the King*, however, what is he like? Some readers believe that when Creon replaces Oedipus as king he should appear more aggressive and forceful than when he left the city. He should seem arrogant and self-confident—much like Oedipus was at the beginning of the play. These readers go on to explain that even good and kind men like Creon become corrupted and cold when placed in positions of power. It's certainly true that in *Oedipus at Colonus* and especially in *Antigone* Creon appears as a tyrant. But he does return at the end of *Oedipus the King* as a stabilizing force to help Thebes regain prosperity now that Oedipus' sin has been purged.

Which theme seems most important to you: the dangerous effects of power, or the need for a nation to reform itself? In all three plays you are repeatedly asked if Creon is a cruel or a fair ruler, a cruel or a fair human being.

Iocaste (Jocasta)

Sophocles gives very little detail about Iocaste. You learn that she married Oedipus because he solved the riddle of the Sphinx and was made king of Thebes as a reward by the gods. Early in *Oedipus the King* you see her trying to mediate between Oedipus and Creon when they quarrel: She appears to be a kind, gracious, and caring wife.

It's important to remember that Iocaste is an older woman, one who was once beautiful and charming. She fell on difficult times when her first husband, Laios, was murdered. Left alone to rule Thebes, she was lost and confused in political matters. She asked her brother, Creon, to share her rule of Thebes, and was obviously happy when Oedipus solved the riddle of the Sphinx and became her second husband. Some readers see her as a weak, dependent woman, but others see her as a tragic figure who fell in love only to learn, too late, that her husband was her son.

When Oedipus demands to see the shepherd who witnessed the murder of Laios, Iocaste agrees without hesitation. Innocently, she has no reason to suspect that Oedipus is her son until the truth is revealed by the herdsman. Although she is a queen, Iocaste doesn't exercise her right to rule. She prefers to let Oedipus make decisions, and she never questions his judgment. But she obviously has a great deal of influence on Oedipus, and he looks to her whenever he needs advice or moral support.

When Iocaste commits suicide at the end of *Oedipus the King*, she does so calmly and without regret. Her suicide is stoical; she welcomes death as a just punishment for having married her own son. You may feel pity and sorrow for Iocaste in spite of her abandonment of and subsequent marriage to Oedipus. But some readers also see her death as a warning not to question the truth of prophecy and the oracles, the messages of the gods. Does Iocaste refuse to believe the oracles because she's foolish or because she's blinded by her love for Oedipus? You decide which interpretation you think fits the theme of the play.

Antigone

The women in the Oedipus trilogy are almost background figures. They react to events, but do not cause events to happen. (This is not true of Greek drama in general, or of all of Sophocles' other plays.) The women have feelings, but they are predictable feelings appropriate to their time and place.

Antigone is something of an exception to this rule. As befits her, she is a loving and loyal daughter and sister. And it is precisely this loyalty that makes her an active rather than a static figure—and, indeed, makes it possible for an entire play to revolve around her. She insists that sometimes justice is more important than law. Creon is perfectly within his rights to forbid burial for Polyneices, but she simply cannot stand by and allow this to happen. No matter what he has done, he is her brother. (She is consistent: she never abandoned Oedipus either.) She arranges for him to be buried, knowing full well the consequences of her actions. In this sense, she is as much a heroic figure as any of the men.

Messengers

The Greek playwrights used messengers to tell the audience what happened offstage. These traditional carriers of news usually told of the murder, violence, or catastrophe that the audience hadn't seen during the play. For example, it is from the messengers that we learn of Polybos' death, Iocaste's suicide, and Oedipus' blinding. In the Greek plays messengers generally were anonymous characters who related facts without offering judgments.

Messengers were usually young men who came running on stage, like marathon runners, to speak long monologues directly to the audience. They were a favorite character of the Athenians because they heightened the tension of the play and provided dramatic spectacle. You need to think of the messengers as "general delivery" men, bringing messages to present to the characters on stage. The fact that Sophocles uses two messengers in *Oedipus the King* is rather unusual. You should keep in mind, however, that the first messenger comes from Corinth with news of Polybos' death, and the second messenger comes from the palace to inform us of Iocaste's suicide and Oedipus' blinding. It would not have been reasonable for one messenger to come from Corinth and also be part of Oedipus' household. The second messenger from the palace was needed to give us an intimate look at Iocaste's suicide and the blinding of Oedipus. The long account of events happening offstage gives the second messenger an opportunity to describe horrible deeds that the playwright didn't want to show the audience, and also adds to the tragic appearance of Oedipus when he stumbles from the palace later.

In *Oedipus at Colonus*, there is only one messenger, as usual. Although Oedipus announces onstage his impending death, it occurs offstage, so you know that it has actually happened only when the messenger appears with the announcement.

In *Antigone* Sophocles again employs only one messenger, this time to tell everyone about the deaths of Antigone, Creon's son Haimon, and Creon's wife Eurydice.

Chorus

Like Teiresias, the Chorus acts as "ideal spectator." Think of the Chorus as a jury. It is a group of twelve or fifteen wise and honest men ("elders") who listen to the facts presented. When the verdict is reached at the end of *Oedipus the King*, it is presented as objective truth, based on the evidence the Chorus has seen or heard. The Chorus is expected to express opinions, question the characters, and to offer advice when requested. (In this sense the Chorus has the opposite function of the messengers.) It speaks in a solemn, dignified tone, and moves in circular patterns while chanting or singing. As a general rule, the Chorus rarely disagrees with the views expressed by the leading characters.

The Chorus is an important part of any Greek tragedy; listen carefully to what it says. Its speeches set the tone of the play, and it never leaves the stage (reminding you that Oedipus' private tragedy has public dimensions). As the plays develop, the Chorus directs audience attention to important ideas expressed. It also warns and reminds characters of the consequences of their actions. The classical Chorus observes what is said and done and then interprets the meaning for the audience. In particular, you should accept its comments as objective truth. The Chorus doesn't judge Oedipus until all of the evidence has been presented.

Pay special attention to the changing moods and attitudes of the Chorus. When it speaks directly to the audience, it is presenting moral and ethical issues. Its judgments represent the basic standards and principles against which all people, including Oedipus, Creon, and Antigone, should be judged. Notice also the odes sung by the Chorus. These lyrical songs help to summarize the plot, comment on the action, and build the play to a climax. The choral odes further help to set the mood of the play, and help the audience understand the emotions of the characters.

Other Elements
GREEK THEATER

There are certain traditions of the Greek theater that can be seen in the Oedipus trilogy. Let's look at some of these.

Classical actors wore masks to suggest the characters they were playing. Men played all the roles in the play, because the Greeks thought it was undignified for women to appear onstage. (This attitude prevailed even in Shakespeare's time, 2000 years later.) An actor might play more than one role. In *Oedipus the King*, for example, while the actor who played Oedipus couldn't play anyone else (Oedipus appears in every scene), the actor who played Creon (who appears only in the first and last scenes) could have doubled in smaller roles like the first messenger or the shepherd. A third actor could have played the roles of Teiresias, Iocaste, and the second messenger. Since they all wore masks, the audience wouldn't notice that Creon had suddenly become a shepherd.

The Chorus was not considered part of the acting ensemble; its role was to chant, sing, or dance as part of the artistic development of the story, and it stayed in a separate area of the stage. These performers may have worn masks as well, but historical sources suggest they were graceful, dignified dancers, who used their own faces to express the changing moods and attitudes of the scenes.

Sophocles made some radical innovations in the use of the Chorus. He increased the traditional number of the Chorus from twelve to fifteen. He also introduced dirgelike instrumental music, probably played on a flute or lyre, to underscore the choral chanting and singing. In other Greek drama, the Chorus usually commented only on the action, or provided transitions between scenes. In *Oedipus the King*, however, Sophocles gave the Chorus a much more active role, as the "ideal spectator," and as the voice of the Theban citizens. The relationship of the Chorus to Oedipus will therefore be an important gauge of his moral progress throughout that play.

GREEK DRAMATIC THEORY

The greatest statement of classical dramatic theory was written by Aristotle in *The Poetics*. He cites the Oedipus trilogy as the best example of Greek tragedy, noting the brief scenes, choral odes, and simple poetry. Aristotle also sets forth some basic elements of tragedy, all of which are brilliantly demonstrated by Sophocles.

The tragic hero According to Aristotle, Oedipus is a tragic hero because he is not perfect, but has tragic flaws. Aristotle points out that Oedipus' tragic flaw is excessive pride (hubris) and self-righteousness.

Aristotle also points out certain characteristics that determine a tragic hero. Using Oedipus as an ideal model, Aristotle says that a tragic hero must be an important or influential man who commits an error in judgment, and who must then suffer the consequences of his actions. The tragic hero must learn a lesson from his errors in judgment, his tragic flaw, and become an example to the audience of what happens when great men fall from their lofty social or political positions.

Watch for these characteristics of the tragic hero to reveal themselves as you read the plays. Oedipus begins as a respected, admired ruler. At the end of *Oedipus the King* he has been stripped of his political power, blinded himself, and exited humbly as a most pitiful creature. What imperfections in his character lead to such a tragic downfall? What were his errors in judgment that resulted in his loss of prestige and respect? What lesson can you learn from his "reversal" in fortune?

Catharsis Aristotle said that a tragedy should move the audience by depicting suffering and pain. The Greeks felt that the audience could learn a moral lesson from seeing a noble man suffer, especially if he learns a lesson from his pain. Psychologically, the effect of this is to produce a climax of tragic pain, after which the audience feels purged, as if they had gone through these events themselves and learned the lesson from firsthand experience. This is supposed to cleanse their souls.

The unities   Because Greek drama was staged without a great deal of spectacle, it appeared natural that the script should also be written in a simple, direct manner. The Aristotelian tradition was to have a "unity of time," in which the playwright included action or events that could logically have taken place in only twenty-four hours. There was also a "unity of place," in which the playwright limited the action or events being described to one locale or setting. The unities dealt with only actual events the audience saw while seated in the theater; dialogue could therefore fill you in on events that happened years earlier or in another city. Watch how Sophocles uses dialogue to tell the story of Oedipus' entire life, one episode at a time. What the Athenian audience would have actually "seen," on the other hand, would have held rigidly to the tradition of the classical unities: One crucial twenty-four-hour period of time in the life of Oedipus or Antigone, who do not leave Thebes in the course of the play.

Although at first glance these unities seem like artificial restrictions, they serve an important dramatic purpose. First, they heighten the emotional intensity of the play. Second, they help to build suspense and intrigue. Third, they limit the scope of the play and focus directly on the main character. (This creates a third unity, "unity of subject.") Fourth, the unities direct audience attention toward the moral of the play by revealing that your lives are as brief as a fleeting day, and you must consider the moral consequences of who you are, here and now.

SETTING

Oedipus the King has one setting, the exterior of Oedipus' palace at Thebes. *Oedipus at Colonus* is set "in the open air," just outside Colonus (near Athens). And *Antigone*'s set is the exterior of Creon's palace at Thebes.

As far as sets or scenery go, there was none to speak of. The exterior palace scenes would have had three doors through which characters entered and exited the stage, as well as an altar. *Oedipus at Colonus* would have given hints—a statue of Colonus to indicate the general location, a rock here, a shrub there. Several steps down led to the orchestra, where the Chorus was located.

There was no curtain to drop between scenes; the passage of time had to be indicated in the play's dialogue, and actors carried torches if it was necessary to show that it was night. (Plays were performed outdoors, in daylight.) There were no special effects; since the Greeks felt that their scripts were sacred, spectacular visual effects would have seemed sacrilegious. The simplicity of the staging and acting was meant to encourage the audience to pay serious attention, using its imagination to fill out the dramatic reality.

THEMES

1. UNCERTAINTY OF HUMAN DESTINY
The plays trace the downfall of Oedipus from a position of wealth and power to a position of despair and sorrow to a position of inner peace. In the beginning Oedipus seems to be a child of fortune who

gained a kingdom by solving the riddle of the Sphinx. In the middle he appears to have been irrevocably doomed by a prophecy before he was even born. And by the end he has found a sort of contentment as he dies with his beloved daughter Antigone by his side. Oedipus' unforeseen reversal of fortune suggests we cannot accurately predict our future—or escape our past.

2. THE ROLE OF FATE

The exact nature of fate, the uncontrollable forces that influence us, is clearly shown in the role that the gods play in revealing the truth of the oracle's prophecies to Oedipus. Although he does all he can to live honestly and avoid the crimes prophesied for him, Oedipus can't escape the relentless fate that pursues him. Creon tries to manipulate fate in his favor, but he fails. Inevitably the oracle's prophecies are fulfilled.

3. SPIRITUAL BANKRUPTCY OF THE STATE

Oedipus' downfall symbolizes the spiritual bankruptcy of the state. Sophocles meant this to pertain not just to the Thebes of the play, but also to his contemporary Athens. The plague that begins the play is viewed as a punishment from the gods, and only when the sins of Oedipus have been punished and purged is Thebes restored—for a time—to spiritual harmony. The loss of the city's spiritual faith is seen in Oedipus' denial of Teiresias' power to predict the future, and in Iocaste's refusal to believe in the ability of prophets to speak for the gods.

4. EXCESSIVE POWER AND PRIDE

Oedipus and Creon share the same tragic flaw. They refuse to compromise or to humble themselves before others. They stubbornly refuse other characters the right to express opinions different from their own, and they abuse their power to force others to accept their points of view. Oedipus is so arrogant and self-confident that he even challenges the will of the gods. This leads directly to his downfall, and he is harshly punished.

5. THE SEARCH FOR FINAL TRUTH

All the characters in the plays search for a final truth of some kind to guide their lives. The most obvious search for truth is Oedipus', but even the minor characters are looking for answers to the meaning of life. The herdsman, for example, has waited many years to reveal the truth of Laios' murder, and is finally given the chance to tell his story when Oedipus summons him to Thebes. Even Iocaste is given the opportunity to discover the truth of Oedipus' early years before he became king of Thebes. The Chorus, too, is searching for a truth—the moral lesson to be learned from Oedipus' tragedy. Teiresias alone stands as a figure who can see truths hidden from all but the gods.

6. SACRIFICE AND SALVATION

Several characters are willing to sacrifice themselves to save Thebes from destruction or for what they believe is right and just. Creon, for example, is ready to die in order to save the city. Teiresias offers to have himself killed when Oedipus suspects him of betraying the trust of the sacred city of Delphi. Iocaste hangs herself to save her honor. Oedipus blinds himself for murdering his father and marrying his mother, but will not die until he has paid for his sins, to save the city. Antigone dies because she insists on giving her brother Polyneices a proper burial.

7. WISDOM THROUGH SUFFERING

Another theme is that suffering leads to wisdom and self-knowledge. Although the ways of the gods are sometimes harsh and cruel, Oedipus finally recognizes and accepts the oracle's prophecy as it was predicted at his birth. You hear the wisdom he gained from his suffering when he prays to the gods for forgiveness and humbly asks for mercy at the conclusion of *Oedipus the King*.

IMAGERY

Several images appear frequently in the plays to call attention to the development of the story. For example, fire and water—associated with the birth of the god Dionysus—are used to suggest the "raging passion" and "cooling reason" that divide Oedipus' personality. When he acts in haste or with anger, for example, Oedipus speaks in images that suggest fire. When he pauses to consider his actions or reflect on his decisions, Oedipus speaks in images that suggest water.

Also pay attention to Sophocles' use of the image "ship of state." When this image appears, Sophocles is comparing Oedipus as ruler to the captain of a ship. We use this same image today when referring to the president as head of state. The image suggests that a ruler is in command of a vessel, and that it is his responsibility to navigate the ship, or state, to safe ports. When the captain is unreliable or irresponsible, the ship of state will flounder, and may even sink.

Sophocles also frequently uses images of blindness and sight. The image of blindness plays a major role in expressing the spiritual theme of the plays. Parallels are drawn between being physically blind and spiritually blind, especially in comparing Oedipus and Teiresias. For example, Teiresias is physically blind but can "see" the awful truth of Oedipus' birth and the oracle's prophecy. Oedipus, even though he has physical sight, is spiritually blind to the truth about his murder of Laios and marriage to Iocaste. When the truth is finally revealed to him, Oedipus physically blinds himself, but is finally able to "see" the spiritual truth of the gods. In *Oedipus at Colonus* Sophocles explores the image of blindness in more detail. He shows you the blinded Oedipus living his life in exile and acquiring wisdom and self-knowledge.

LANGUAGE AND STYLE

The Greek playwrights wrote in poetry to give dignity and beauty to their dramatic creations. Unfortunately you are working with a translation of the original Greek language. Many versions—some in poetry and some in prose—of the Oedipus story now exist. You may, for example, be reading the Peter Arnott translation, which is a poetic version of the original story. Or you may be reading Paul Roche's translation, which is a line-by-line transposition of Roche's words for Sophocles' original words. You may even be reading the William Butler Yeats translation, which omits 90 of the last 226 lines of the play, credits some of Oedipus' dialogue to other characters in the play, and places certain speeches by Iocaste 100 lines from their original position in Sophocles' script!

Obviously you can anticipate some differences of opinion and interpretation of a play or a character whenever you are reading a translation. Although each translator captures the basic episodes of the play, there may be individual scenes or lines of dialogue in one edition that don't agree at all with other translations. More likely than not, this difference in translations will provoke a great deal of discussion, and may even result in interesting and perceptive interpretations of the play.

This guide uses translations of *Oedipus the King* and *Antigone* by Dudley Fitts and Robert Fitzgerald, two leading theater scholars and historians. The translation of *Oedipus at Colonus* is by Robert Fitzgerald alone. These were chosen because their simple prose dialogue is clear, direct, and dramatic. They also re-create what theater scholars believe is the flavor of the historical style and form in Greek tragedy. Fitts and Fitzgerald don't indulge in the high-sounding language, archaic words, pretentious dialogue, or literary obscurities that are found in other English-language versions of the plays. For your first reading of a famous Greek tragedy, these modern prose translations are a good choice.

The Stories

OEDIPUS THE KING

Oedipus the King begins at the point in the legend where Oedipus, king of Thebes, is trying to rid his city of the plague. Oedipus sends Creon to the oracles at Delphi to find out the solution to the city's woes. Creon is away for quite a while, and he returns accompanied by Teiresias, the blind prophet. They report the oracles' statement: the plague will end only when Laios' murderer is discovered. Sophocles shows you the chain of events that finally unmasks Oedipus as the murderer. That Oedipus acted unknowingly is irrelevant; he feels he must be punished for his heinous crime, and so in his despair he blinds himself. His wife and mother Iocaste hangs herself. Creon ascends the throne of Thebes, and Oedipus goes into exile.

PROLOGUE

The play begins with the Prologue, a tradition in classical Greek theater. Here the dramatic tone of the story is set and a problem is presented. The audience gets basic facts that are necessary to understand what's going to happen next.

At the beginning of the Prologue a crowd of suppliants bearing crowns of olive leaves and fig branches lie despairingly on the steps of the palace of Oedipus, king of Thebes. Their low moans of sorrow drift upward to the palace windows and draw Oedipus forth. He stands on stage, a towering figure, compassionate and understanding. He addresses his loyal followers grandly, confidently, as if they were his children:

> tell me what preys upon you,
> Whether you come in dread, or crave some blessing:
> Tell me, and never doubt that I will help you
> In every way I can.

A priest of Thebes, wise and solemn, slowly advances toward Oedipus. He is hesitant and cautious before this famous person. You realize that Oedipus isn't looked up to just because he's the king; he's genuinely admired and respected. The priest speaks urgently, informing the king that the city of Thebes, once prosperous, is now in ruin. A mysterious, unnatural plague has settled on the countryside, causing unborn children to die, and the cattle to get sick. Perhaps today you'd look to science for a solution to such a calamity. In Sophocles' time, however, there would have been no doubt in anyone's mind that there are religious causes for this misery.

It appears that these people have come to seek comfort and advice from Oedipus, the "wisest in the ways of God." Oedipus, after all, solved the riddle of the Sphinx. Surely, they feel, Oedipus can now find a remedy for the plague. Only Oedipus can restore Thebes to its former glory.

NOTE: The Sphinx was a monster who proposed a riddle to the people of Thebes and killed all who could not solve it. Oedipus gave her the correct answer, and she killed herself. The riddle asked by the Sphinx was: "Who moves on four in the morning, on two at noon, and three in the evening?" The correct answer, given only by Oedipus, was "man." He moves on all fours as a baby, walks upright in his prime, and uses a cane as an old man.

Oedipus is genuinely touched by the spectacle of his suffering "children." He promises to investigate the unknown cause of the deadly plague. In fact, like any effective leader, he's already taken action. He explains that he's sent Creon, brother of his wife, Queen Iocaste, to the sacred city of Delphi to ask the oracles for a pledge that might yet save the city from destruction. Oedipus is worried, however, that Creon has been gone too long. Just then, Creon rushes in with a troubled expression on his face.

NOTE: The Greeks believed in the oracles, who lived in Delphi, about fifty miles from Thebes. Creon's hurried there to ask the holy oracles to interpret what the plague meant.

At first Creon hesitates to speak before the anxious crowd. He suggests to Oedipus that it would be more appropriate if they withdrew to the palace to speak in private. Oedipus, however, commands Creon to let everyone hear what the oracles have said. Creon unfolds a tale of woe and misery in guarded, almost evasive language:

> The god commands us to expel from the land of
>   Thebes
> An old defilement we are sheltering.

NOTE: Oedipus has taken a risk here. Some readers think that he is showing excessive pride and self-confidence when he demands that Creon tell the crowd what the oracles have said. Others think that he is merely being a fair, honest ruler who deals openly with his subjects. Think about our own political leaders: A public press conference, with its impromptu questions and answers, is far riskier than a prepared speech delivered from notes.

Oedipus is stunned by Creon's speech. What defilement does he mean? At the king's urging Creon continues his story in plain, direct words:

>   It was
> Murder that brought the plague-wind on the
>   city.

This revelation drops like a ticking bomb among the Theban citizens. But Oedipus, a man of action, immediately presses for more specific information. He demands that Creon name the man responsible for the crime, but Creon can only repeat the story of the crime as it was told to him by the oracles: Laios, who was king of Thebes before Oedipus, went on a religious pilgrimage. On the road he was brutally attacked by a band of highwaymen. The former king and his servants, save one who escaped to spread word of the crime, were killed or left to die. Directly following Laios' murder, new problems arose in Thebes, and there was never a chance to hunt down the killers and avenge the murder.

Oedipus is outraged by this tale, and he resolves to avenge the murder of Laios personally. He has several motives for this: 1. personal safety: the murderer could reappear at any moment to kill him as well; 2. public duty: as king he must avenge the city and the city's god; 3. moral concern: for everyone's sake it will be good to be rid of evil.

NOTE: Sophocles is already developing his definition of the relationship between the individual and the state. A stable political order benefits each person living in it. Sophocles is also developing his definition of a king's responsibility to his kingdom. Oedipus' personal and public roles can't be separated, for both affect his subjects. Think of how you react today when a politician is caught in a scandal. Why do you become more outraged by that than when private citizens commit similar crimes?

The Prologue concludes, however, with a note of joyous celebration. The suppliants and priests gather up their ceremonial olive boughs and fig branches. They rejoice, certain that Oedipus will expose the murderer and save the city from inevitable ruin. Oedipus himself exits proudly, reminding his followers that he will do all he can to unmask the murderer:

We shall be saved—or else indeed we are lost.

Imagine the tone of voice you think Oedipus uses here—urgency and doubt, or self-confidence. Some readers see him as arrogant, too sure of his power—and heading for a fall. Others say he's a concerned, strong leader, at the peak of power, just before cruel fate pulls him down.

Up to this point the play has simply created the central situation. Remember that the audience in Athens knew the story of Oedipus from the legend, just as you might know the legend of Johnny Appleseed or Superman. What they were looking for was not a tantalizing plot, but a commentary on human nature, politics, and ethical questions. The rest of the play, therefore, will identify the murderer and punish the crime.

NOTE: Remember that the legend of Oedipus began before he was born with a prophecy that he would kill his father and marry his mother. Watch how and when Sophocles brings in this important information. Sophocles skillfully weaves together the present and the past as Oedipus nears his fateful doom. In the scenes that follow, watch how Sophocles uses dramatic irony to foreshadow the tragic decline of Oedipus: Look for those speeches by Oedipus in which there seems to be an extra meaning that you understand because you know the story, but Oedipus doesn't understand yet.

PARADOS

The Prologue is traditionally followed in Greek tragedy by the Parados, where the Chorus enters. As the "ideal spectator" of these events, this group of actors represents the community and speaks directly to the audience.

NOTE: At first the Chorus moves slowly in one direction to recite its lines of verse (*strophe*). Then it abruptly turns and moves in another direction to recite another set of lines in the same poetic meter (*antistrophe*). The dramatic effect of this suggests that a decision has to be made. The Chorus is presenting several possible solutions to the dilemma expressed in the Prologue. The members speak in unison, but the "voice of the people" includes several viewpoints.

First the Chorus restates poetically that Thebes is dying because of the unexplained plague; that the gods must swiftly—but mercifully—intervene to save the city. The Chorus then prays to the gods, asking them to relieve the city from despair. The first antistrophe concludes with a direct plea for Athene and Artemis, goddesses of mercy, to save the city again.

NOTE: Athene and Artemis once before intervened to save Thebes from destruction by barbarians. Notice that the Chorus unquestioningly turns to the gods to help solve the mystery raised by the oracles' message to Creon. This is important later on because both Oedipus and Iocaste will question the power of the gods and their holy prophets to solve such mysteries. When the Chorus hears that, it will begin to doubt Oedipus and his wife, and then they will have to win back the favor of the people.

The second strophe and antistrophe again offer prayers and praise to the gods if they will intercede to save Thebes and end the people's afflictions. This second and concluding strophe and antistrophe, however, ask the gods to be tender and compassionate.

Already, a seed is planted in your mind—perhaps Thebes will have to pay a high price for relief.

The Chorus works itself up to a frenzied climax in the third strophe, forcefully recalling that the plague resulted from the shameful actions of a "besieger," the murderer of Laios. The Chorus calls for a violent revenger:

> Destroy our enemy, lord of the thunder!
> Let him be riven by lightning from heaven!

The final antistrophe rises to a note of religious ecstasy. The Chorus declares that when the plague ends, the faithful must be prepared to greet the moment with celebration. As the Chorus turns to exit, it leaves the audience a final warning. The gods will:

> Whirl upon Death, that all the Undying hate!
> Come with blinding torches, come in joy!

NOTE: Traditionally, the Chorus was impartial and didn't participate in the action of the play. Sophocles, however, gives the Chorus a more active role in this play; later the Chorus will confront Oedipus and pass moral judgments on the reasons for his fate. Pay particular attention to the Chorus' choral songs and dialogue with Oedipus, and trace the change in its mood and its attitude toward him. After all, the Chorus (like the citizens it speaks for) is affected by the king's actions. This is the tragedy of Thebes, as well as of Thebes' king. It should also make you think about how any community—ancient Athens or your own city today—suffers when its leaders go wrong.

SCENE I

Oedipus enters from the palace and delivers a speech of passion and power. He recalls how he came as a stranger to Thebes. He promises personally to provide relief from all the evils that have beset the land. In the middle of his long speech Oedipus' anger rises, and he proclaims a curse on the murderer of Laios. He further decrees that anyone hiding the murderer will be driven from the land and denied all religious rites of prayer and sacrifice—thus damned eternally. Oedipus concludes by pledging that the murderer will be "consumed in evil and wretchedness."

NOTE: Sophocles uses dramatic irony skillfully in Oedipus' speech. Oedipus unknowingly pronounces a curse on himself; you can see that it will be *he* who is driven from the city, once he is unmasked as the murderer of Laios. Some readers think that Oedipus' outburst shows only his arrogance and pride. Others think that he is unwisely acting in haste before all the facts are known. But the greatest irony is that he has assumed the role of one of Laios' children—without knowing that he *is* Laios' son. He says that he must take the son's part and avenge the murder.

Oedipus plays the detective, looking for missing clues that will reveal the murderer. His pursuit of the criminal is similar to a modern "whodunit" like Agatha Christie's *Murder on the Orient Express*, and the surprising ending is just as shocking.

The Chorus interrupts Oedipus to suggest that a clairvoyant be sent forth to investigate the mystery. Oedipus—always one step ahead—tells the Chorus that he has already sent Creon to seek out the prophet

Teiresias. He's worried, however, because Creon hasn't returned yet. Although Oedipus believes in oracles or prophets, he decided to summon Teiresias only because Creon suggested it. This is an important point to remember. Oedipus' later suspicion of a conspiracy between Creon and Teiresias is the result of their late arrival in Thebes.

Teiresias finally arrives alone. The Chorus, signifying the public respect for this man, hails him with cheers as he is led to the stage by a young child. Your first impression of him, therefore, is a puzzling mix of power and helplessness. The blind prophet retreats as Oedipus moves toward him. At first Teiresias is stubborn and refuses to answer any of Oedipus' questions. Oedipus is puzzled by this personal insult to him as king, and in turn reacts with disrespect to Teiresias. When Teiresias does speak, it is in riddles and jingles. He tells Oedipus that "there is no help in truth," and that only misery can result from his knowledge.

Oedipus' tone is bold and almost blasphemous: this would be like doubting the pope, and you can imagine the loss of respect that Oedipus suffers in the eyes of the audience. But Oedipus is so angry and frustrated that he can think only that Teiresias and Creon have planned to disgrace him here in front of his people. He even accuses Teiresias of being behind the murder:

> You planned it, you had it done, you all but
> Killed him with your own hands.

Teiresias responds by saying that Oedipus himself is the "pollution" of Thebes. Taken aback, Oedipus doesn't understand what Teiresias has said. Is this another riddle? But Teiresias repeats it and adds, even more specifically, that Oedipus is the murderer he seeks. When Oedipus demands that Teiresias deny what he has said, the holy prophet refuses. But Oedipus cannot accept this baffling truth. His anger turns to the absent Creon, and he accuses Creon and Teiresias of plotting to seize power by discrediting him.

Speaking as the ideal spectator, the Chorus interrupts and reminds Oedipus and Teiresias that they have both spoken in anger. The Chorus also suggests that the only important matter is to decide how the gods' will can best be served.

The argument continues, however, and Teiresias reminds Oedipus that although he is a king, he is not a god. The prophet is only speaking for the gods, and he reprimands Oedipus for his "blindness" in this matter.

NOTE: Sophocles appears to have been fascinated with the struggle between earthly and divine authority. In *Antigone* Oedipus' daughter is put to death for refusing to obey a law passed by Creon, who is king of Thebes after Oedipus. The moral argument presented by Sophocles is whether man should be ruled by the laws of the king or the laws of the gods and their prophets. Keep this theme in mind as you consider the role that Teiresias plays in revealing the truth to Oedipus.

Before his exit Teiresias reminds Oedipus that he once solved the riddle of the Sphinx. The holy prophet offers Oedipus another riddle to solve. The mysterious riddle describes the murderer of Laios. He is a "blind man, who has his eyes now." Teiresias says that when this murderer is discovered he will tap the earth with his staff (like a blind man's white cane), and he will be to his children

Brother and father—the very same; to her
Who bore him, son and husband—the very
   same
Who came to his father's bed, wet with his father's
   blood.

This prediction seems like an ominous, convoluted echo of Oedipus' birth prophecy.

The first scene ends abruptly with the exit of Teiresias. Oedipus is left alone on stage to think about the riddles Teiresias gave him to solve.

NOTE: What is important here is that Teiresias has exposed the truth that Oedipus is responsible for the plague. But until the whole story is pieced together, Oedipus will not accept this. Why not? Some readers think he is arrogantly rejecting the message of the gods; others think he loves power too much to give it up. Yet others say it's natural for Oedipus to cling to a faith in his own virtue. He has been a good man and a wise, fair ruler; he has not intentionally sinned. Perhaps inside he is beginning to worry and doubt, but in his public role as king he must appear strong and confident.

Examine the role that irony plays in pointing to Oedipus as the murderer. Sophocles doesn't tell you much about Oedipus' past before his arrival in Thebes, at least not yet. More information of Oedipus' past will be revealed later when the first messenger and the shepherd tell their stories. But you need to be aware early that Sophocles is deliberately withholding information to heighten the tension and the suspense. You may remember the whole story, but the characters on stage don't have all the pieces of the puzzle yet.

From this point on in the story Sophocles shifts the emphasis of the plot. Oedipus begins to become more interested in finding out about his own past than in finding the murderer of Laios and ending the plague. Teiresias' puzzling riddles have confused Oedipus, and he now begins the search for his true identity. In his pursuit Oedipus exhibits a rash and impetuous nature that leads to his downfall. Notice also the conflict between Oedipus' desire to uncover the truth and his horrified refusal to draw the inevitable conclusions from what he learns.

ODE I

Choral songs (*stasima*) were an important part of traditional Greek tragedy. They were used as interludes or transitions between scenes. The Chorus may have chanted, recited, or spoken the choral songs in a rhythmic pattern as it moved around the stage in a semicircular pattern.

The first choral song has two strophes and two antistrophes. The Chorus is uncertain, and hesitates to support either Oedipus or Teiresias in the argument that concluded the previous scene. The Chorus is consoled, however, by recalling that the murderer is even now being pursued by Oedipus, and predicts that the Furies will also track down the desolate villain responsible for Laios' death. There's no way the murderer will escape punishment.

NOTE: The Greeks believed that the Furies would pursue those who committed crimes or offenses against man and nature. The Furies were supposed to exact blood for blood, when no human avenger is left alive. They were particularly concerned with injuries

done by one member of a family to another. Sophocles' mention of them here foreshadows what will
happen to Oedipus in *Oedipus at Colonus*. In that play
the Furies torment Oedipus, reminding him of his fate
and refusing to let him forget his past actions. In this
sense they resemble a "conscience" that never allows
anyone to forget the horrible deeds he has committed.

In a second strophe and antistrophe the Chorus
continues to express confusion. After weighing the
evidence, however, the Chorus declares its faith in
Oedipus. The main reason for trusting him rather
than Teiresias is personal past experience: Oedipus
solved the riddle of the Sphinx. The Chorus concludes
that Oedipus, the city's savior, can't be doubted until
he is proved wrong. Distinct memories resurface:

> I saw him, when the carrion woman faced him of
>   old,
> Prove his heroic mind! These evil words are lies.

The final choral ode is important to the development
of the story because the Chorus supports Oedipus'
side of the argument with Teiresias. Later, when
Oedipus is discovered to be the murderer of Laios, the
Chorus admits its error in supporting him. Like any
citizen committee responsible for evaluating evidence
and making a decision, the Chorus can make a mistake. But it can also recognize that mistake and
reverse its opinion. Watch now as the tide of opinion
turns gradually away from Oedipus and toward the
truth of Teiresias' prophecy.

NOTE: As a dramatic device, the first choral ode
helps to suggest the passing of time from one scene to
another. Remember that traditional classical plays had

to describe events that took place within a twenty-four-hour period. The choral ode, therefore, signals to the audience that a certain number of hours have elapsed between the scenes. This choral ode also allows the Chorus to point out to the audience things to watch for in the events to come. Sophocles used this opportunity to heighten the tension and suspense of the play.

SCENE II

Creon now enters to address the Chorus and the audience. He had been absent when Oedipus accused him and Teiresias of conspiring to seize power; this is his opportunity to speak when Oedipus is not present. Creon begins protesting his innocence and denying that he is part of any conspiracy. Tension builds as Creon personally attacks the reputation and moral character of Oedipus. This would be a lot like the "character assassination" tactics that followed the downfall of Richard Nixon. Creon speaks in anger but also out of fear. Why? He is innocent of conspiracy but perhaps doesn't trust Oedipus to behave fairly. This is the first time you've felt Oedipus' ability as a leader questioned. Already his power is starting to disintegrate.

Creon's outrage reaches its climax when he asks the Chorus if Oedipus has lost his mind, almost replaying the previous scene:

> But you were watching him! Were his eyes steady?
> Did he look like a man in his right mind?

The Chorus is surprised by Creon's outburst. It admits that there's no way of knowing whether Oedipus was seriously accusing Creon or just spouting off in anger. But the Chorus reminds Creon that Oedipus is king and that it is impossible to judge the behavior of great men. This is an important point to consider. The Chorus may be saying that Oedipus has a right to say and do whatever he chooses because he is the king, an absolute authority. Or the Chorus may be saying that for the good of the state no one should question the actions of a ruler.

NOTE: Some readers look to this first part of the scene to prove that Creon is jealous of Oedipus' political power and is actually plotting against him, asking for support from the Chorus. Others suggest that the Chorus is telling Creon to reserve judgment, that only the gods can judge a king. Pay close attention to the tone of Creon's outburst here because later in the play, when he becomes king of Thebes, he will treat Oedipus like he thinks he is being treated now.

The mood of the scene is quickly shattered when Oedipus enters from the palace. Oedipus obviously has had time to think about the conspiracy he suspected in the first scene; further thought has confirmed his suspicions, however. His first words to Creon are an accusation. He calls Creon a murderer and demands that he confess to having killed Laios.

Creon is stunned by this. He doesn't understand why he should now also be a suspect in the murder. Oedipus' principal argument is that if Teiresias knew the brutal facts of Laios' death, he should have spoken out earlier. Why did he wait until now to accuse Oedipus? Oedipus asks. Was he bribed to do so by Creon? Oedipus' logic may be off-base here, but Creon is taken off guard just now, and he tries to meet the accusations.

The only answer Creon can think of to defend Teiresias is that Teiresias is a man who holds his tongue when he has no facts to go on. For himself, however, Creon can think of several reasons why this accusation is false. Turning toward the audience for support, he lists four reasons why he wouldn't be Oedipus' rival for power.

NOTE: It was customary for citizens to defend themselves in court in Athens. All of these reasons would have appealed to the Athenian audience, because they are the basic democratic principles of Greek society and government. This approach by Creon would be like a modern politician referring to the Declaration of Independence to justify his refusal to accept public office.

Creon presents his defense by saying: 1. he never wanted a king's power, only his individual rights; 2. he would refuse the office of king because he never wanted to be a slave to policy; 3. he has no need of personal "honors," only his honorable reputation; and 4. he hates anarchy and could not support any man who did.

Turning back to Oedipus, Creon encourages the king to visit the priestess at Delphi to hear for himself that Creon quoted her accurately. After that, Creon says, if Oedipus still thinks there is a conspiracy, he can sentence Creon to immediate death. This is a brave offer to make, but Creon has worked up his sense of innocence—and perhaps his anger—to a bold pitch.

The Chorus interrupts, encouraging Oedipus to consider the wisdom of Creon's words. For the first time the Chorus suggests that Oedipus is not acting like a wise and honored ruler. But Oedipus ignores the Chorus' advice. Instead he demands that Creon be put to death as a "symbol" of what treason means. As his anger mounts Oedipus says that Creon is "evil incarnate," and should pay for his treason with his life. Surprisingly, Creon remains calm throughout this outburst. He doesn't interrupt again to protest his innocence. His only reaction is to say to the audience that Oedipus is a "fool." His self-control throws Oedipus' irrational reaction into a bad light.

Mercifully, the heated argument is broken off when the Chorus announces that the queen, Iocaste, is approaching; perhaps she'll be able to make peace between her husband and her brother. This pause in the action of the story gives you a moment to look at what is happening. Oedipus has lost control; he scarcely seems capable of reason or logic. Creon emerges as a sympathetic character who is being abused and misjudged. Iocaste's arrival, however, presents you with some hope that the argument will be resolved without bloodshed.

Why is Oedipus behaving so rashly? In a matter of a few hours he has dramatically changed from a compassionate ruler, interested in solving the mystery of the plague, to a ranting hothead, intent on destroying Creon. Imagine yourself in Oedipus' position. Teiresias' troubling prophecy is still fresh in his mind. Perhaps Oedipus is now beginning to suspect that he himself played a role in the murder of Laios—and it bothers him.

NOTE: Most critics point to this scene between Oedipus and Creon as the first indication that Oedipus is hastening toward his ultimate downfall. He is quarrelsome and angry; he refuses to compromise or to see Creon's point of view. His suspicious nature makes him question everyone's opinion but his own.

Later you may want to compare this scene to the final scene between Oedipus and Creon to see how each man has changed as the story unfolds and the truth is revealed.

Iocaste has been drawn to the scene by the men's loud voices, which she overheard in her bedroom. Imagine Iocaste's entering here like a worried mother who has heard her children fighting over some trivial matter. She tries to persuade Oedipus and Creon to be calm and behave themselves. But Oedipus refuses to listen to her and again demands the death of Creon.

One unique feature of Iocaste's scene with Oedipus and Creon is the insertion of two strophes to separate the lines of dialogue. Remember that strophes were used before in the Parados, chiefly to suggest the indecision of the Chorus. Here, however, they are used to plead with Oedipus. The Chorus begs Oedipus to open his mind to Iocaste's views and to respect Creon's protests of innocence. When Oedipus refuses to change his position, the Chorus attacks his vanity and laments his once-noble character. It also reminds him that there's trouble enough in Thebes without the king causing more.

Urged on all sides, Oedipus finally agrees to spare Creon's life, but insists that he leave Thebes at once. He remains angry toward his brother-in-law, though, vowing to hate him as long as he lives. Creon, on the other hand, shows no bitterness toward Oedipus. He keeps his poise and noble stature, in contrast to Oedipus' ugly rage.

When Creon is banished from Thebes, it appears to Oedipus that the problem has been solved. Oedipus seems convinced that Creon was responsible for the plague, and that Creon and Teiresias really were plotting to seize his throne. You could expect Oedipus and Iocaste to return to the palace at this point. But if they did that the play would be over. Sophocles introduces more conflict by having Iocaste ask the Chorus what Oedipus and Creon had been arguing about.

Iocaste's question is ironic because it causes her to learn information that will throw her life into a tailspin. Iocaste refuses to accept the Chorus' account of a conspiracy between Creon and Teiresias. She innocently asks Oedipus to tell her what Teiresias said that provoked such anger and confusion. Before Oedipus can relate the story, the Chorus interrupts and pleads with Iocaste to let well enough alone. Tension rises as Iocaste, despite the warning, presses on. Iocaste's innocent question prompts Oedipus to reveal the prophecy made by Teiresias. If Iocaste had not been so inquisitive, Oedipus would never have mentioned Teiresias' visit. Of course, Iocaste is only trying to find out what Oedipus and Creon were quarreling about. She has never seen or heard them argue before, and is disturbed that her husband and brother have parted as enemies.

Ignoring the pleas of the Chorus to remain silent, Oedipus tells Iocaste that Creon must have hired that "damnable soothsayer" to make false accusations against him. Surprisingly, Iocaste is delighted to hear this news. She tells Oedipus to set his mind at rest. She can offer proof that soothsayers shouldn't always be taken seriously.

NOTE: Iocaste's role in this scene is very important to the development of the plot. Although she has acted out of innocence, Iocaste encourages Oedipus to deny the wisdom of soothsayers and to pursue the truth on his own. Inevitably, of course, this will lead him to discover that he is the murderer. Remember this scene when Iocaste appears later and again innocently suggests that Oedipus send for the shepherd who was witness to the attack on Laios. She is the key to the story; without her unknowing help, the awful truth of the prophecy could not be exposed.

Now Iocaste gives her "proof" that soothsayers can't be taken seriously. She begins a long story by telling Oedipus that, years ago, an oracle once told Laios, her former husband and king, that he would be killed by his own son. Believing the oracles, Laios pierced his infant son's ankles together and had him taken into the countryside to be left to die. Later, when Laios was an old man, he was killed not by his son but by barbarians, while he was on a holy pilgrimage. This, Iocaste claims, should be enough to convince anyone what prophets and prophecies are worth. But her innocent anecdote is full of a significance she doesn't notice.

When Iocaste finishes her story there is a moment of stunned silence. Oedipus suddenly demands to know *where* and *when* Laios was killed. He is strangely frightened by Iocaste's response that Laios was killed a short time before Oedipus came to Thebes, at Phokis, where the road divides the towns of Delphi and Daulia. Imagine the anguished look on Oedipus' face as he tries to understand the story he just heard. A shadowy memory crosses his mind; he senses that something is wrong. He suddenly cries out:

Ah, what net has God been weaving for me?

Does he already understand the connection, or is he just unsettled by vague fears? Either way, from this point on Oedipus is obsessed with the specific details of Laios' death. He demands to know what Laios looked like, and what his features were like. When

Iocaste tells him that Laios was similar in height and weight to himself, Oedipus trembles with fear. Something is stirring his memory. Perhaps he is recalling the "curse" he had pronounced on the murderer of Laios in the previous scene. He admits as much, and more, when he says that he himself "may be accurst/ By my own ignorant edict," and that he is "not sure that the blind man can not see." Perhaps Teiresias really was speaking truth.

NOTE: Most readers point to this recognition scene as the first time Oedipus suspects himself as Laios' murderer. Keep this in mind as Oedipus has other scenes of recognition later in the play. Why does it take Oedipus so long to realize the truth? Is he too proud and self-confident to see his role in Laios' murder? Or is he so frightened that he keeps hoping to avoid the truth by dismissing it? You need to ask yourself these questions as you try to understand his later refusals to come to grips with the prophecy given him by Teiresias.

Iocaste also appears to be frightened in this scene. Perhaps she is just reacting to Oedipus' fear, but she tries to calm him by revealing that the story she told of Laios' murder was hearsay. The person who told her about the incident was a faithful servant, the sole survivor of Laios' band of men who were attacked by barbarians. The servant had escaped and returned to Thebes several months after the murder of Laios. But when he saw Oedipus on the throne, for some reason the servant begged Iocaste to send him away from the palace. She did so without question, and the servant left for the wild frontier to live out his life as a shepherd.

Again, Iocaste's innocent information triggers an urgent response from Oedipus. He insists that the shepherd be brought to Thebes immediately. Iocaste hesitates. Perhaps she's simply upset by Oedipus' reaction; perhaps she, too, is beginning to sense that these stories all fit together in some disastrous way. You might even wonder whether Iocaste knows more than she's telling, to protect herself or Oedipus. The mystery has mushroomed, becoming a complicated tangle of details to unravel. And the characters' tense, anxious reactions only impress on you how much they have at stake here.

Now it's Oedipus' turn to tell a long story. At last you learn about his life before solving the riddle of the Sphinx and becoming king of Thebes. Oedipus says he was born in neighboring Corinth. His father was Polybos and his mother was Merope, wealthy citizens of Corinth. He recalls that one night at a feast, a drunken friend of the family blurted out that Oedipus was not his father's son. Although he was still a young child, Oedipus was troubled by the accusation, as probably any child would be; he spent hours thinking about what the man had said. As he grew older, lingering doubts remained about his parentage. Finally, when the suspicions and doubts built up into an obsession, Oedipus left his parents and went to Delphi to consult the oracles about his birth. The oracles told him he would

> lie with [his] own mother, breed
> Children from whom all men would turn their
>   eyes;
> And that [he] should be his father's murderer.

When he heard this prophecy, Oedipus fled Delphi and vowed never to return to Corinth to tempt the oracles' prediction. Oedipus tells Iocaste that as he was wandering along the road to Thebes he met a hostile band of travelers at the crossroad near Cithaeron. One of the men—who resembled Iocaste's description of Laios—struck Oedipus on the head as they passed. Infuriated, Oedipus picked up a club and struck the old man with such force that he died. Although the old man was paid back, Oedipus was so furious at the insult he also attacked the other men in the band—killing them all, he thought, with savage blows of the club. When his anger ceased, Oedipus continued his journey to Thebes. It was there that he met the Sphinx, solved the riddle, and was named king. His marriage to Iocaste soon followed, and he saw it as a reward from the gods for his courage and wisdom.

NOTE: The first part of Oedipus' narrative is the historical legend familiar to the Athenian audience. They knew, for example, that Oedipus was rescued by a shepherd and later taken to Corinth, where he grew up thinking Polybos and Merope were his parents. They also knew that he might murder Polybos and marry Merope as the prophecy had suggested. The second part of Oedipus' narrative, however, mixes historical legend and Sophocles' own addition to the story. Sophocles added three elements to the legend: 1. a detailed account of Oedipus' unpredictable tendency toward violence; 2. Oedipus' admission that there was a similarity between the old man he killed and Laios; and 3. the suggestion that Oedipus recognizes, for the first time in the story, his personal involvement in the murder of Laios.

At the conclusion of his story Oedipus recoils in horror at what he himself has said, and admits to Iocaste

> Think of it: I have touched you with these
>   hands,
> These hands that killed your husband. What de-
>   filement!

At this point Oedipus finally acknowledges that he must be the murderer of Laios. He is, therefore, the cause of the plague (notice he uses the same word "defilement" that the oracles used in telling Creon what caused the plague). The original problem is solved, then; but before you can even think about whether Oedipus should exile himself, you are urged on by a host of other unsettled questions growing out of the original mystery. What is this prophecy about Oedipus? Whose son is he? What happened to Iocaste's baby, and why did the shepherd beg to leave Thebes when he saw Oedipus? Sophocles uses this moment to slow the action of the play so the audience can consider these questions. Just as Oedipus pauses to pray to the gods to exile him from Thebes, the Chorus moves toward the audience to speak.

The Chorus begs Oedipus not to flee Thebes, reasoning that he should hear the shepherd tell his story of the murder of Laios before assuming any guilt. Apparently the Chorus is still somewhat on Oedipus' side. Perhaps his mood has changed, from anger to personal concern, and the Chorus' sympathy shifts back toward him, forgetting his rash banishment of Creon.

Taking heart from the Chorus' speech, Oedipus suggests a possible "happy ending" for himself. He reasons that if the former servant, now living as a shepherd, can prove that Laios was killed by a gang and not by a single man, then Oedipus still could be innocent. He's immediately persuaded by his own argument, and is anxious that the shepherd be sent for at once. This moment may revive your hope to

avert tragedy, but it's an ironic hope. This shepherd's
news will reveal more than Oedipus bargains for.

Iocaste is uneasy, unwilling to pin everything on
the shepherd's story. Somehow her reluctance sharp-
ens your fear that his answers will not be comforting.
She tells Oedipus that the shepherd is now an old
man and can't possibly remember the details of the
murder. Furthermore, the shepherd has already told
everyone that Laios was killed by a gang, so he isn't
going to change his story and now say Laios was
killed by a single man. Further, she protests loudly,
the shepherd couldn't show that Laios' death fulfilled
the oracles' prophecy, because

> My child was doomed to kill him; and my child—
> Poor baby!—it was my child that died first.

Iocaste's anxiety may show her weakness and confusion, or it may show her love for Oedipus, rising to a
desperate pitch.

Oedipus rejects Iocaste's views, saying that even
though she may be right, the shepherd is the only
man alive who can shed any light on the circumstances of Laios' death. Iocaste reluctantly
agrees, and a servant is sent to bring the shepherd to
Thebes. Oedipus and Iocaste retreat to the palace to
wait. The Chorus moves toward the audience to sing
the next choral ode.

The scene began with a confident and arrogant
Oedipus having complete faith in his innocence and
righteousness. Now Oedipus suspects that he may
have been guilty of the murder of Laios. He is less
sure of himself; his pride and self-confidence are
shaken. But he's still hunting down the truth, while
Iocaste watches fearfully. Imagine their moods as they
disappear into the palace. You turn to the Chorus, to
mull over what has just happened.

ODE II

The second choral ode explores some of the moral questions raised by Iocaste in the preceding scene. The Chorus debates the nature of the prophecy and the role that oracles play in interpreting the will of the gods. As the Chorus chants, its tone is solemn, expectant, and quietly reverent. There are frequent images that suggest "holy law," "sacred wood," and "holy things."

In the first strophe the Chorus pleads with the gods to provide some moral direction. It prays for strength to help maintain the "laws of the pure universe." It is puzzled by the "ways of right," and needs guidance in unraveling the mysterious oracles and prophecies.

After the Chorus addresses the gods, it turns its attention to Oedipus. First it chastises him as a tyrant. Then it scolds him for his pride. Finally it criticizes his recklessness. The Chorus is obviously displeased with the actions of the king, and yet it prays that the gods will protect him, because he is the "wrestler for the State." You realize that Oedipus may have human faults, but his failures will have greater impact because he is the king.

A second strophe continues the moral argument, stressing that the "holy laws" of the gods must be preserved above all. The Chorus openly condemns haughtiness and the "high hand" of all those who abuse the power they wield. The Chorus predicts—ominously—that anyone who questions the gods will be "caught up in a net of pain." (Remember Oedipus' lament about "the net" the gods were weaving for him?)

The Chorus then solemnly turns to address the audience, saying that some will lose faith in the oracles and prophecy, but the faithful will stand steadfast in their religious beliefs. Finally the Chorus predicts that those who deny the oracles and prophecy are ignorant of the ultimate truth of the gods.

The second choral ode raises several important issues. First, the Chorus tells the audience that if the holy oracles and prophecy are proved wrong, then the gods themselves may be suspect (this would be an earth-shaking concept for the Greeks). Second, the Chorus tells the audience that anyone who questions the holy oracles and prophecy should be doubted as well. Third, the Chorus tells the audience that men are blind to the truth of oracles and prophecy because they no longer have faith in the gods.

NOTE: Remember that when the Chorus speaks directly to the audience it is addressing *all* Athenians, forcing those who may be guilty of these same sins to take heed of Oedipus' imminent downfall. Even though Oedipus is not present on stage at this time, the Chorus is indirectly speaking about him. Its warnings and prayers are part of Sophocles' moral message to the citizens of Athens; dramatically, the Chorus also heightens the suspense by hinting at what is to follow in the play. Even when you know the legend you may be on the edge of your seat, waiting to see what new chunk of dreadful knowledge will be thrown at Oedipus.

As the ideal spectator, the Chorus defines public opinion of Oedipus; it is beginning to express doubts about Oedipus' innocence. Perhaps the people don't support Oedipus anymore, and are preparing to abandon him to his own fate. On the other hand, the Chorus speaks frequently about oracles, prophecy, and the gods; perhaps it is acknowledging that Oedipus is caught up in a web of cruel destiny from which he cannot escape. He did not know Laios was his father, and killed him only by accident. He had no idea Iocaste was his mother. Have you ever been accused of doing something, or hurting someone's feelings, when you had no control over what you were doing? That's Oedipus' problem, only on a much more intense level. Now you will see how the gods—and his mortal countrymen—judge him for it.

SCENE III

The third scene begins with Iocaste entering alone from the palace. She immediately falls to her knees in prayer to the gods. This is a most unusual entrance. Earlier Iocaste had questioned the power of the oracles and prophecy. Why is she now praying to the gods? Perhaps she knows more than she's told you; perhaps Oedipus told her something new while they were alone in the palace; or perhaps she is simply terrified and desperately trying to placate the gods.

Iocaste's prayers are similar to those of the priest in the Prologue. She enters as a suppliant carrying sacred incense; her prayers ask for guidance and understanding. Then she expresses her concern for Oedipus, who appears to be "not himself." It's a frightening experience to see someone you love suddenly act like a stranger. Iocaste's heart is heavy with fear as she approaches the altar. She pleads softly with the god Apollo, the spirit of help and reward, to restore Oedipus to his former self and to save the people of Thebes from destruction. She, too, is aware of the public dimensions of her husband's personal troubles.

Iocaste's prayers are interrupted unexpectedly by the hurried arrival of a messenger from Corinth. The messenger, overjoyed, boasts that he brings good news for Oedipus. Polybos, Oedipus' supposed father, has suddenly died and the people of Corinth wish Oedipus to become their king.

Iocaste is delighted to receive this news. She interprets it as a token from the gods she has been praying to, that the oracles were wrong in their prophecy. Quickly she sends a maidservant to the palace to fetch Oedipus. Iocaste then speaks to the audience, saying that because the death of Polybos came while Oedipus was in Thebes, this proves that the oracles can't be taken seriously. Loudly rejoicing, Iocaste gives thanks that Polybos died by another fate. She's eager to believe the gods were wrong, because it will clear her husband.

NOTE: At first glance the entrance of the messenger offers new hope to resolve Oedipus' doubts about his part in the oracles' prophecy. But this is just a device by Sophocles to give some false relief to Oedipus. Ironically, this same messenger will later reveal other facts about Polybos and Oedipus that will shatter Oedipus' illusions. In one way the role of the messenger is to heighten your expectations that Oedipus will be spared. But in another way the messenger is used by Sophocles cruelly, to delay the inevitable revelation of the truth, and to string out the suspense.

Oedipus rushes in to ask why Iocaste called him. She tells Oedipus that Polybos is dead. At first Oedipus can't believe the news. He asks the messenger if his father's death was by treason or by an attack of illness. The messenger says that Polybos simply died of old age.

Imagine the conflicting emotions in Oedipus' heart. This news of a painless death cheers him for the moment; then he is sad to realize that Polybos, whom he loved, is dead. All of this shows a sensitive, loving, compassionate Oedipus, to counteract the raging hot-head you saw banish Creon. Oedipus then rejoices out loud when he realizes that he hasn't been involved in the death, and that the oracles have been proven wrong. In spite of his grief, Oedipus is human enough to react with self-interest.

Oedipus' joy is short-lived, however. He recalls his widowed mother, Merope; he asks Iocaste if he should return to Corinth and risk fulfilling the second half of the oracles' prophecy: marrying his mother.

Iocaste laughs at Oedipus' fears, saying that all men, in their dreams, "have lain with their mothers!" (Her laughter here is a prime example of dramatic irony.) Oedipus, still troubled, tells Iocaste he wishes his mother had also died. Iocaste is amazed and shocked by Oedipus' attitude, but he reminds her of the oracles' "dreadful saying."

NOTE: As a result of Iocaste's innocent remark that all men have dreamed of sleeping with their mothers, there have been many Freudian interpretations of this play. Sigmund Freud, the founder of psychoanalysis, saw the characters of Oedipus and Iocaste as person-ifications of a primal human desire when he wrote about the "Oedipus complex" in his essay "The Inter-pretation of Dreams."

In Sophocles' time the notion of incest was strictly frowned on. Oedipus even mentions this in the play.

True, there were classical examples of men know-ingly committing incest with their sisters or mothers, but the subject would have been too scandalous for a play. (Remember, the drama was part of a religious rite.) Oedipus didn't *know* Iocaste was his mother when he married her; she was presented to him, almost like a gift, when he solved the riddle of the Sphinx. There is no indication or evidence that their marriage was anything other than a social or political necessity that restored a powerful male figure to the throne of Thebes after the death of Laios. As an exercise in creative interpretation, you might look for veiled mentions of the "Oedipus complex" in the play, to see if you detect subtle inferences of Oedipus' hatred of his father and sexual attraction toward his mother.

At this point the messenger tries to ease Oedipus' mind. He pleads with Oedipus to forget his fears and to be cheered by the news of Polybos' death. He adds that any fears of fulfilling the prophecy are nonsense because Polybos was not his father.

The messenger now turns to address the audience. The role of the messenger in Greek tragedy was to give information, so Sophocles uses him to fill in more of the events in Oedipus' life before he solved the riddle of the Sphinx and was made king. The messenger confesses that he was the same man who found Oedipus as an infant and took him to Corinth as a gift to the childless Polybos and Merope. The messenger concludes by saying that the infant he found and called Oedipus (which means "swollen foot") was actually given to him by a shepherd said to be one of Laios' people.

As Iocaste grows noticeably frightened and turns pale with fear, Oedipus demands that the shepherd be brought to him. The Chorus informs Oedipus that the shepherd he is seeking is the same shepherd he has already sent for about the murder of Laios. The "net" begins to draw tighter. Iocaste, in a daze, pleads with Oedipus to drop the whole matter. She rushes from the stage screaming

Let us have no more questioning!
Is your life nothing to you?
My own pain is enough for me to bear.

While some readers see Iocaste as a hysterical female here, others see her as a woman with deep emotions, overwrought by her intuitive sense that disaster is near. Again you wonder if Iocaste knows something that she's refusing to admit.

Oedipus, on the other hand, is now firmly resolved to pursue the truth of his birth. He thinks that Iocaste is distressed by the fact that he might have been born "humbly" and therefore is not suitable as a husband to a queen. He apparently has no thoughts of what the messenger's story means regarding the oracles' prophecy. He directs a servant to find the shepherd and bring him to Thebes. The Chorus steps forward to address the audience.

The Chorus speaks to the audience in a quiet and hushed tone. It whispers that it is afraid for the safety of Iocaste. Why has she fled in such a "passion of sorrow"? What does her dreadful silence mean? Oedipus interrupts to say that Iocaste has fled because she fears his birth was base, and she wishes to avoid the public scandal. This hardly seems fair to Iocaste. That dangerous self-confidence may be rising in Oedipus again, blinding him to the truth Iocaste has sensed.

NOTE: Sophocle's dramatic skills are at their highest point in this scene. His use of the messenger diverts attention away from the murder of Laios and in the direction of Oedipus' birth. The use of the messenger also permits Sophocles to bring in more of the legend to the plot. Some readers believe that Sophocles uses the messenger as a symbol of death, summoning Oedipus to the horrible truth by offering him the truth of his birth. Other readers see this scene as

crucial in revealing Oedipus' part in the murder of
Laios, with the messenger forcing Oedipus to seek
out the shepherd. Ironically, Oedipus might not have
been so eager to send for the shepherd if the messenger hadn't told him the fellow had knowledge of
Oedipus' past. Now the king is determined to speak
to this humble subject. Like Iocaste, you have a sink-
ing feeling that Oedipus won't hear anything good
from the shepherd.

ODE III

This choral ode is the shortest in the play. It is also
the most hopeful and optimistic in tone. Why is it
placed here? Perhaps Sophocles is continuing the
"false hope" that Oedipus can escape his fate. The
lack of tension and anxiety in the choral ode might
also suggest that you need to pause here and consider
what has just happened. Sophocles could even be
deceiving you, diverting your attention from the real
issues of the play: Who is the murderer of Laios? Who
is responsible for the mysterious plague? Who will
unmask the villain who lives in Thebes?

The Chorus is optimistic that the shepherd will
reveal that Oedipus was born of a noble race. This
would calm Iocaste's fears—at least her fears as Oedipus interprets them. You know, however, that this
isn't the real issue.

The Chorus is full of joy and praise as it tries to
guess the origin of Oedipus' birth. Some say he was
born of nymphs; some say of the god Apollo; and
other say of Hermes. The frenzy of the Chorus
reaches a climax when it concludes that Oedipus must
have been born of the great Dionysus, the sacred god
of fertility (and, coincidentally, the god honored by
this dramatic festival!). Once more you are being led

by the Chorus to expect a happy ending for Oedipus. By comparing Oedipus to the nymphs, Apollo, and Hermes, the Chorus is painting a picture of a noble, royal, and wise king who must have been the child of the gods.

NOTE: Sophocles is masterful in distracting you and the audience. The classical tradition in tragedy insisted that the audience weep and wail at the end of a play, as a means of cleansing their souls. In a modern sense, you do the same thing when you cry at the conclusion of a sad film; don't you feel better afterward? In order for the full impact of the tragedy to be felt, Greek playwrights usually included diversions— songs or brief episodes—just before the final scene. They felt this heightened the tragic effect of the final scene, when the painful climax of the tragedy would be revealed.

SCENE IV

The fourth scene brings all of the traditional legend and the oracles' prophecies to a climax. It reveals, without doubt, that Oedipus is the murderer of Laios and is married to his own mother. The brief scene also sets in motion the dramatic resolution of the tragic events that have happened so far, especially the fate of Iocaste.

The first five lines are significant. Oedipus enters from the palace in a hurry. He looks into the distance and "sees" the shepherd approaching several miles away. He even describes the shepherd in detail. Before this scene, Oedipus was described as "blind" by Teiresias. Perhaps Oedipus' sight here shows that he is finally beginning to "see" the reality of his actions. On the other hand, it could be one last ironic reminder that Oedipus can see physically, but is morally blind. Keep the eye imagery in mind as you read this scene. It will soon be brought to a climax when Oedipus blinds himself.

The shepherd arrives in Thebes but is hesitant to speak. (Remember how Teiresias refused to speak back in Scene I?) The shepherd denies ever having seen the messenger from Corinth and can't remember giving him an infant child. The messenger reminds the shepherd that they spent several months together tending sheep in the mountains, and the shepherd finally admits that it is true.

Oedipus draws nearer to listen to the shepherd and is fascinated by what he hears. The shepherd and messenger quarrel about the "little child," and each accuses the other of telling lies about the episode. Sophocles is deftly drawing out your curiosity.

Oedipus suddenly grows angry (you've seen this side of his temper before), and he threatens to kill the shepherd if he doesn't tell the truth. The king orders his servants to bind the shepherd until he reveals all he knows about the little child he reportedly gave to the messenger. When the shepherd is bound to a post, he turns to the Chorus for help, crying out

If I speak the truth, I am worse than dead.

The shepherd is finally threatened into submission, and quickly blurts out that the little child he gave the messenger many years before was Laios' child.

A hush falls over the Chorus when the truth of Oedipus' birth is revealed. Oedipus stands rigid, paralyzed with fear. The old shepherd slowly turns and faces the audience to tell the whole story of his part in the events. Oedipus was the son of Laios and Iocaste; he was given to the shepherd to be killed because of a prophecy that said Laios' child would kill his father and marry his mother. But the shepherd had pitied the little child and gave him to the messenger from Corinth to spare his life.

The shepherd then realizes what he has said and what this truth means for Oedipus. He concludes his story by saying gravely

> If you are what this man says you are,
> No man living is more wretched than Oedipus.

Oedipus now knows that the prophecy has come true. With a final cry of despair, he rises and rushes toward the palace.

NOTE: Now that Oedipus knows the truth, you should pause to consider what possible punishment is due. Surely the penalty for having murdered his father and married his mother will be severe. Athenian law condemned parricide and incest; Oedipus has broken the most sacred of moral laws. Others would have been put to death or exiled for such crimes. Will Oedipus be punished—even though he acted in innocence and without knowledge, even though he was the victim of a prophecy he couldn't control?

Some readers think Oedipus should be judged leniently. But others point out that he is the king and as such should be an example to his people. Can they respect him anymore? Could they ever trust him again if he weren't punished? Think about the standards you hold for political figures today; don't you expect your leaders to be model citizens? As this scene ends you should anticipate some punishment for Oedipus. The Athenian audience would have expected justice to be served. They would also have wondered why Oedipus could so easily solve the riddle of the Sphinx, but not the mystery of his birth or the oracles' prophecy. This may prove more than anything how much of life is controlled by the gods; they allowed Oedipus to guess one riddle and become king, just so he would ignore the other riddle and bring himself to ruin. As you read on consider: Was Oedipus too arrogant and self-confident to suspect his role in Laios' death? Is his excessive pride the cause of his tragic downfall, or would he have been doomed anyway? Do you pity him, or do you feel he's getting what he deserves?

ODE IV

The somber Chorus sings the final choral ode. It warns the audience to prepare for more suffering and despair. Then it tries to stir your sympathy for Oedipus' tragic circumstances. After all, you're reminded, man's fate is uncertain and unpredictable. The chorus asks for compassion for Oedipus, the unwilling victim of a cruel fate.

The first strophe moans for the sad plight of Oedipus. There is a note of hopelessness in the song when the Chorus reflects on what has happened. In a direct reference to Oedipus, it sobs that his splendor is gone and his days of happiness are numbered.

The first antistrophe again summarizes the early period of Oedipus' life. The Chorus points out that Oedipus had a mind like a "strong bow," and that he "stood like a tower" against the enemies of Thebes. (Note the warlike images. Athenians still could recall the terror of foreign invasion—a good king would have been a good defender, in their eyes.) The Chorus concludes by comparing Oedipus' strength and determination to the gods themselves. Even now Oedipus still seems "divine" to his people.

In contrast, the Chorus then laments that Oedipus is now the most "pitiful" of men. It cautions the audience to view Oedipus' change of fortune as an example of what happens when men are the victims of fate. It also questions Iocaste's role in Oedipus' tragic downfall, asking why she remained silent in the face of the truth. The Chorus is taking a sterner, judging tone.

In the second antistrophe the Chorus assumes responsibility for what has happened to Oedipus. His people were also blind to his fate and couldn't see the truth. The Chorus points out that "justice" must prevail eventually, yet it pleads with the audience to have sympathy for Oedipus and to forgive him.

It is important to understand the sympathetic tone of the fourth choral ode. It sets the audience up for several responses: 1. It suggests that Oedipus is innocent of knowingly murdering his father and marrying his mother. 2. It offers the hope that the gods will intervene and save Oedipus from punishment. 3. It prepares the audience to pity Oedipus in his final entrance as a ruined hero. 4. It allows the audience to judge for themselves if Oedipus' decision to blind himself is just payment for his actions.

NOTE: In the play that follows this one, *Oedipus at Colonus*, you see what happens to a man who has been arrogant enough to question the will of the gods or the prophecy of the oracles. The extent and results of Oedipus' self-knowledge would have been seen immediately following this play, when *Oedipus at Colonus* was presented. Pay careful attention to Oedipus' final words in the concluding scene of this play to understand *why* he chooses to blind himself and take his daughter Antigone with him to Colonus.

EXODUS

The last episode of the play is divided into five individual segments. It represents the longest "resolution" scene in classical Greek tragedy.

NOTE: Traditionally the Exodus serves two purposes. The choral recessional signals the conclusion of the play's action. It also concludes the moral action of the play, as the Chorus' last speeches define the moral theme.

Sophocles, however, delays the exit of the Chorus until all threads of the plot have been resolved. Oedipus is given an extended opportunity to accept the judgment of the gods. He is also given a long time to prepare for his future life as a blinded, but now wiser, man. This is one reason for the length of the Exodus. But are there other reasons for prolonging it?

Some readers suggest that the extra length of this Exodus allowed Sophocles to underscore the moral lesson more fully for the Athenians watching the play. Some readers suggest that Sophocles is concerned with shifting the emphasis from Oedipus the *murderer* to Oedipus the *outcast*. Still others suggest that Sophocles is preparing you for the basic themes that appear in *Oedipus at Colonus*.

Regardless of the interpretation you prefer, you will see that Oedipus is purged of self-righteousness and excessive pride as the play ends. You can feel pity and sorrow for him because he has been the victim of fate. It's important that you think about how he punishes himself, and why he's willing to suffer for his actions. This will all fit into the moral theme stated by the Chorus in the last four lines of the play.

The first segment of the Exodus begins when a pale second messenger enters from the palace. The messenger, who is from Thebes, laments the horrors and the sorrows that have taken place so far in the play. He then tells the audience of new horrors and sorrows that have taken place behind the palace doors.

NOTE: Properly speaking, this messenger is not a runner bringing a letter from far away; he's a household servant, stepping out to relate the latest events in this public and private tragedy. The Greeks avoided showing violence onstage, so Sophocles must use a "reporter" to tell you about acts too shocking to be seen.

What is the effect of keeping bloody scenes offstage? Perhaps the Greeks wanted to preserve the solemn, dignified air of their drama (part of a religious festival). Today you are accustomed to dramatized violence on TV and in movies; death and mutilation onstage perhaps wouldn't shock you so much. But there is a powerful dramatic value in keeping violence just out of sight. Instead of being shocked by a gory reenactment, you are forced to imagine these dreadful acts as the messenger tells you about them. You do not turn your eyes away, but become drawn in to the horror of what has just happened.

The messenger simply says that Iocaste is dead; she killed herself in her bedroom. As the Chorus moans in sympathy, the messenger elaborates on Iocaste's death. She stood by her bed and called out to Laios as she wailed aloud about

> the double fruit of her marriage,
> A husband by her husband, children by her
> child.

Then she untied the belt of her dressing gown and made a noose around her neck. Standing on a chair in the center of her room, Iocaste prayed to the gods for forgiveness, and kicked the chair away. Oedipus rushed in and found her hanging in the air, her body swaying from the "cruel cord" she tied around her neck.

The messenger is so overcome with sorrow that he pauses to sob. After a moment he continues. There is still more grief in store. He tells you that Oedipus cut Iocaste down and held her in his arms. Then he ripped the golden pins from her gown and plunged them into his eyeballs, screaming out in his agony

> No more shall you look on the misery about me,
> The horrors of my own doing! Too long you have known
> The faces of those whom I should never have seen,
> Too long been blind to those for whom I was searching!
> From this hour, go in darkness!

The Chorus recoils in dismay, but the messenger continues his story, piling one grim detail on top of another. Oedipus struck at his eyes many times until the blood splattered down his face and beard. Finally he burst his eyeballs and "red hail" filled the room. The messenger turns to the audience and says that Oedipus is even now calling for someone to lead him to the gates of Thebes. He has decided to exile himself from the city so that no one can look on the man who murdered his father and married his mother. The messenger warns the audience that this tragic spectacle is so horrible it would "crush a heart of stone."

Now you are prepared to see Oedipus yourself. The central door of the palace slowly swings open and Oedipus staggers to the stage. Blood is still dripping from his face, and he leans heavily on a wooden staff for support. The terrifying sight of the once proud and noble king entering in bloodstained shame shocks the Chorus, and this reaction suggests how the audience should react. Turning back to Oedipus at last, the Chorus asks the audience what madness or demon could have caused Oedipus' life to be filled with such punishment. It seems to be even greater than his crime deserves. In the quiet moment that follows, Oedipus moves slowly toward the audience to speak.

Oedipus is a changed man. Some see him as shattered, a ruin of himself; others find something grand in his humility. He pleads with the gods to help him find a safe haven in the world. He prays for understanding of what the gods have done to him. Yet he still curses his fate. He wonders what will become of him and his children.

Oedipus and the Chorus exchange dialogue in a series of strophe and antistrophe. In these alternating lines of speech Oedipus and the Chorus set forth the moral lesson of the play. You learn what Oedipus has learned from his fate. This exchange also helps Oedipus and the Chorus reconcile their past differences of opinion and move toward a single spiritual view.

Oedipus speaks first in each strophe and antistrophe. He recalls with sorrow the events of his life and thanks the Chorus for being faithful and supportive even now. He takes responsibility for blinding himself, saying he couldn't bear to see "horror everywhere" in his actions. Physically helpless now, he begs the audience to forgive him and lead him away from Thebes. He then laments that he was ever saved from death by the shepherd, saying that if he had died as an infant

> This weight of monstrous doom
> Could not have dragged me and my darlings
>   down.

Notice that he mentions his children, who are inextricably tangled in his fate.

The Chorus speaks last in each strophe and antistrophe. It reminds the audience of the incidents that have led up to the terrible spectacle they now see before them. It declares that Oedipus is a sad example of excessive pride (hubris) that leads to destruction, pain, and remorse. The audience is warned never to commit such fearful acts themselves. Finally, the Chorus questions whether perhaps Oedipus should have killed himself when he discovered his true identity. Surely Oedipus would be better off dead than alive and blind.

In the second segment of the Exodus the Chorus, which is undecided about Oedipus' future, continues to debate the facts of the case. After all, the Chorus must give a final verdict, and it doesn't want to be hasty in its judgment. This allows you, too, to turn over in your mind the significance of what Oedipus has done.

In the third segment of the Exodus Oedipus nobly assumes all responsibility for what he has done. He tells the audience that his sense of moral outrage and repulsion made him blind himself. Self-punishment was necessary, he says, because the horrible crimes he committed against the gods and against the city of Thebes demanded severe penalties. In his eyes at least, his ignorance of his parentage is no excuse for the shameful deeds he performed. Oedipus justifies choosing blindness rather than death by saying

> I could not make my peace
> By strangling my own life.

He has to live in order to suffer, to pay for his sins.

As the Chorus pauses to consider these moral arguments, Oedipus continues to plead his case. Oedipus tells the Chorus that neither his children, the city of Thebes, nor the gods could ever have been purified if he hadn't blinded himself; his public responsibility looms large here. He calls himself a "defilement" for having doubted the oracles' prophecy and pleads with the Chorus to exile him.

Oedipus also addresses the audience and asks for their forgiveness. He unflinchingly lists his crimes: first, marriage to his mother; second, murdering his father; third, the act performed in his mother's bed, which was so horrible no tongue could repeat it. Incest seems to be the worst crime of all in his eyes.

The fourth segment of the Exodus begins with the entrance of Creon. Creon has returned from Thebes to be the new ruler of the city. The Chorus tells Oedipus that Creon is the best one to judge his punishment, because he is the only one left to protect the city now that Iocaste is dead and Oedipus is disgraced.

Here is another moment of dramatic irony in the play. Recall that Oedipus banished Creon earlier and refused to listen to his pleas of innocence. Now Creon is the one who will judge Oedipus and decide his punishment. He seemed like a good man before, but perhaps power will change him. He had a strong sense of justice before, but perhaps that will now make him hungry for revenge on Oedipus.

The first thing Creon does when he enters is to kindly inform Oedipus that he doesn't come to mock or reproach him in front of the Chorus and the audience. His first concern is for Oedipus' suffering, and he orders servants to take Oedipus into the palace as quickly as possible, to make his suffering less public.

Oedipus refuses to leave, however, and bravely asks that Creon exile him to a place where no human voice is ever heard. Creon hesitates to grant Oedipus' request. He says the gods' will in this matter has not yet been revealed to him. Naturally, after what has happened to Oedipus, Creon is anxious not to go against the gods. Ironically, Creon was the one who brought the oracles' message to Oedipus in the beginning of the play. Oedipus reminds Creon that the law of the gods is very clear in this case: the murderer—especially a parricide—must be cast out and destroyed.

Creon finally agrees that Oedipus is correct in his understanding of the gods' law, but he still hesitates to exile Oedipus. Why the delay? Some readers see Creon as a hard but fair judge who is trying to decide the right punishment for Oedipus, which could be death rather than exile. Others see him as a vengeful man who is already becoming a tyrant. Yet others think he can't make up his mind because he's overwhelmed with pity—as the Chorus is.

NOTE: In *Antigone*, Sophocles' play about Oedipus' daughter, this question of Creon's character plays an important role. Creon, now king of Thebes, regrets that he didn't have Oedipus killed when he had the chance. He also blames Antigone for inheriting her father's "stubborn" nature and refusing to honor his laws. He also fears that Antigone is really the ghost of Oedipus, who has come back to haunt him. Eventually Antigone kills herself just like her mother did, by hanging herself.

Before Creon grants Oedipus his wish to be exiled, he asks that Oedipus abide by the will of the gods. Oedipus agrees, but asks for three promises in return.

First, Oedipus begs Creon to give Iocaste a proper funeral. Second, Oedipus pleads to be exiled to the wild hills of Cithaeron, where his father and mother had left him to die as an infant, thus completing the circle of his life. Third, Oedipus asks Creon to take a solemn oath to care for Oedipus' and Iocaste's small daughters, Antigone and Ismene.

As Creon pauses to consider these requests, the Chorus, moved to tears, begins to pray for Oedipus and his children. You can imagine the audience also crying and reaching out to comfort Oedipus in his misery.

Next Sophocles brings on Oedipus' children. This not only increases your sympathy for Oedipus, it also provides a link to the next two plays in this trilogy, where Oedipus' children—especially Antigone— play a greater role.

Whatever you think Creon was planning to decide for Oedipus, public sympathy would be swerved totally to the blinded hero's side, as Antigone and Ismene are led to the center of the stage. The girls don't speak any dialogue, but Oedipus hears them weeping. He clutches his daughters to him, greeting them with the ironic news that he is their "brother." He tells them that when they were born he had no sight, no knowledge that Iocaste was also his mother. But he isn't making excuses for himself. Recalling the agony of his horrible crimes, Oedipus weeps aloud as he imagines his daughters' cursed future. He again begs Creon to be the father of his daughters. Creon takes pity on them and agrees to act as their guardian; he and Oedipus shake hands to seal this solemn pledge. Thankful for this act of kindness, Oedipus immediately offers a prayer for his daughters' happiness.

Creon agrees to send Oedipus away from Thebes at once, hoping time can ease his pain. There is a final, happy reconciliation as Oedipus and his daughters go their separate ways into the palace. As the blinded king exits, ready for his life in exile, he appears to have lost everything. Yet even while you pity him, you can still see that he's a hero. He has faced his tragic punishment with incredible courage; he never held back, but plunged boldly after truth and made no excuses for himself. He has examined the depths of his soul and judged himself honestly. He has put his public duty ahead of his own desires. As he leaves the stage, he is stripped of everything but his own integrity and inner strength. But because he has proven his greatness, you come away admiring him more than ever and trying to learn from his example.

NOTE: Before hearing the Chorus' final judgment, let's pause and consider Creon's role in the resolution of the play. At first glance you might have expected Creon to be bitter or angry when he returned to Thebes as the new king. After all, Oedipus earlier humiliated and disgraced him in front of the citizens of Thebes and wrongly accused him of conspiring with Teiresias. The fact that Creon now treats Oedipus with sympathy and kindness should suggest that he is an honest and forgiving man. Surely with these noble characteristics he will prove to be an excellent ruler.

Some readers suggest that Sophocles paints a sympathetic portrait of Creon here to suggest that the transfer of power will be smooth and efficient. The political order survives, even when a leader is disgraced. Unlike some modern political elections where a victorious candidate pledges to undo his former rival's policies, Creon seems filled with compassion and understanding for his defeated rival. But this is no guarantee that Creon will be a better king. In fact, to some readers he seems less heroic than Oedipus— the good old days of Oedipus' glory are gone forever. Other readers suggest that Creon's nobility introduces a note of hope at the conclusion of the play. They hold the opinion that Creon represents the dawning of a new age of reason and conciliation in the political climate of Thebes. Creon's ability to understand and forgive Oedipus signals that his rule of Thebes will be characterized by fair play, compassion, and compromise.

The final segment of the Exodus summarizes the plot of the story and presents the moral lesson. The Chorus reminds the audience that Oedipus was once a powerful king envied by his followers. Now, however, ruin has swept over him. The Chorus tells the audience to take heed of the example of Oedipus' pride and arrogance in questioning the will of the gods:

> Let every man in mankind's frailty
> Consider his last day; and let none
> Presume on his good fortune until he find
> Life, at his death, a memory without pain.

When they have delivered this final verdict, the Chorus slowly exits in a ritual procession. They circle the holy altar in the center of the stage and then exit left and right in single file. The audience has time to pause and consider the wisdom of what the Chorus has said. Questions of Oedipus' guilt and innocence, power and pride, suffering and sacrifice are still revolving in your mind. The oracles have spoken in this play, and the audience has been shown that prophecy is never to be questioned.

OEDIPUS AT COLONUS

Oedipus at Colonus was constructed when the playwright was in his early 90s. The plot is rather loosely connected in a series of individual episodes and individual song lyrics. There is very little character development because Oedipus, although twenty years older now than in *Oedipus the King*, is basically the same man he always was. He is proud, hot-tempered, rash, impetuous, and quick to anger. There is very little indication that his personality has radically changed in spite of his punishment. Indeed, he appears to have accepted his punishment only because there was no alternative. He continues to insist that he, personally, is innocent of any crime against man or the gods and maintains that the "crimes" he committed were the result of destiny, in whose angry hands he was but a helpless victim.

Oedipus at Colonus revolves around the exiled, blinded Oedipus and his daughter Antigone, who has accompanied her father in his wanderings. While resting near the edge of a sacred grove, Oedipus is discovered by the inhabitants of Colonus. The residents are frightened to discover the identity of their visitor and immediately send for the king, Theseus. Meanwhile, Oedipus' other daughter, Ismene, arrives with the news that Creon, now king of Thebes, is coming to take Oedipus back because the oracles have decreed that the spot on which Oedipus dies is to be forever sacred and holy. When Oedipus refuses to accompany him, Creon seizes Antigone and Ismene as hostages. At this point Theseus enters, stops Creon, and sends soldiers to rescue the daughters.

Oedipus' son, Polyneices, who is marching against Thebes (as he later does in the play *Antigone*) also arrives at Colonus and asks for his father's blessing in the upcoming battle. Oedipus, however, refuses to bless Polyneices and, instead, curses him to a quick death. A great storm arises, at the height of which Oedipus makes his way, alone, into the sacred grove and disappears. Later, a priest enters from the grove and describes Oedipus' final moments before his death. Theseus declares the spot forever sacred, and takes Antigone and Ismene into his protective custody.

Although the play doesn't completely develop the character of Oedipus in his final days, it does provide a moving tribute to the man who, though basically good, was punished by the gods for sins he committed in ignorance. There is a kind of mystical aura surrounding Oedipus and his children in this play, and Sophocles suggests quite clearly that Oedipus has been purified and cleansed of his sins by suffering and sorrow. There are also several mystical scenes that depict Oedipus gaining heroic stature and nobility by enduring his pain and agony. Further, Sophocles appears to sketch a patriotic portrait of Oedipus as a fallen hero who has finally achieved in his death a stature of noble dimension.

SCENE 1

Oedipus, now old and blind, is led into the sacred grove at Colonus by his youngest daughter Antigone. A stranger enters and reveals that the grove is a shrine to the gods, and admission to it is forbidden. Oedipus asks the stranger to bring King Theseus to him, and the stranger departs to consult with the wise elders of Colonus to decide what to do.

CHORAL DIALOGUE

The Chorus enters to express curiosity about the presence of Oedipus in the sacred grove. Oedipus will come out of the grove if the Chorus promises not to harm him. After the Chorus agrees, Oedipus reveals himself and his true identity. The Chorus is frightened of Oedipus and urges him to leave town at once.

SCENE II, CHORAL DIALOGUE, SCENE III

Oedipus begs the Chorus to have pity on him and finally persuades them not to take any action until Theseus arrives. Ismene suddenly rushes in to warn her father that her brothers, Eteocles and Polyneices, have quarreled about who should rule Thebes now that Oedipus is exiled. Eteocles drove Polyneices from the city, and now Polyneices is raising an army to conquer Thebes for himself. In addition, the holy oracle at Delphi has prophesied that whatever city houses the burial place of Oedipus will have good fortune. Both of Oedipus' sons and Creon, king of Thebes and Oedipus' brother-in-law, are planning to take him into custody to secure the good fortune for themselves.

Oedipus curses his sons and Creon for their plans and begs the Chorus to protect him. He promises to give his blessing to them when he dies, and they gratefully accept his offer. After Oedipus seals the bargain with an offering made to the gods, the Chorus pleads with Oedipus to retell the horrible story of his life. He does so in great detail, but protests that he is innocent of any crime because the deeds were done in ignorance and without deliberate, evil intent.

At the conclusion of this story Theseus enters and greets Oedipus with respect and dignity. When he learns the plans of Creon and Oedipus' two sons, Theseus promises to protect Oedipus and his daughters. He also pledges that Oedipus may remain at Colonus until his death.

CHORAL POEM

In celebration of Theseus' pledge to protect Oedipus and his daughters, the Chorus chants a lyrical song praising the beauty of the sacred grove at Colonus and of the Athenian countryside.

SCENE IV

Creon enters the grove to persuade Oedipus to return to Thebes. He tries to convince Oedipus that he is concerned only with his well-being and happiness, and that the people of Thebes are in need of their former king's wisdom and leadership.

Oedipus reacts quickly, telling Creon that he is a hypocrite and a traitor. Oedipus goes on to tell Creon that he knows about the oracles' prophecy, and that he suspects Creon would keep him prisoner on the outskirts of Thebes until he died, and then bury him in the city in order to secure the good fortune promised by the prophecy.

Knowing that persuasion is impossible, Creon has his men seize Antigone. He tells Oedipus that Ismene has already been taken prisoner, and that both daughters will be taken back to Thebes as hostages until Oedipus returns there himself. The Chorus tries to prevent this seizure but is too weak and too old to stop Creon's men. Suddenly, Theseus and his followers appear and rescue Oedipus. Theseus sends his party ahead to rescue Antigone and Ismene, telling Creon that he himself will be held prisoner until the daughters are safely returned to their father.

Creon protests that he is a king and can't be treated this way. Theseus, a king himself, dismisses these arguments and marches off to secure the rescue of Antigone and Ismene. The Chorus consoles Oedipus, who again pronounces his innocence and ignorance of crimes committed against the gods.

CHORAL POEM

The Chorus surrounds Oedipus and sings a song of victory, praying to the gods to support Theseus in his battle with Creon for the rescue of Antigone and Ismene.

SCENE V

Theseus and his followers return happily with Antigone and Ismene, rescued after a bitter struggle with Creon and his band of warriors. Oedipus welcomes his daughters and embraces Theseus, who is now being honored by the Chorus. Suddenly a stranger appears and claims to be a relative of Oedipus. It is Polyneices, who has come to seek Oedipus' blessing before attacking Thebes. Oedipus refuses to speak to Polyneices at first, saying "his voice is hateful to me."

CHORAL POEM

Following a tense argument between Oedipus and Polyneices, the Chorus sings a sad song about the suffering and misery that signals old age.

SCENE VI, CHORAL POEM AND DIALOGUE, SCENE VII

Polyneices finally enters the grove and laments the misery he has caused his father and sisters by not helping them during their long exile from Thebes. He tells his father that he was robbed of the throne by his younger brother, Eteocles. Polyneices now plans to revenge himself by securing an army and attacking Thebes, and he wishes to have Oedipus' blessing because the oracles have predicted that whoever wins the favor of Oedipus will be victorious in the battle.

Oedipus rejects Polyneices' request and predicts that his oldest son will never be victorious in the battle. He further prophesies that both of his sons will be overcome with grief and die on the battlefield. He orders Polyneices to leave Colonus.

Before he leaves, Polyneices begs Antigone to give him a proper burial if he is killed in the battle for Thebes. Antigone promises to honor Polyneices' request, and brother and sister embrace for the last time.

A foreboding crash of thunder interrupts the scene, and Oedipus asks the Chorus to send for Theseus at once. The thunder grows louder as Oedipus suddenly becomes frightened. Antigone sees the concerned look on her father's face and asks what is wrong. Oedipus confesses that his life will soon end and that the thunder is a sign the gods are summoning him to his death.

When Theseus enters, Oedipus calls him aside and warns him to keep secret what he's about to hear. Oedipus leads Theseus to the place where he will die and reveals the "holy mystery" that will benefit Athens after his death. Antigone and Ismene accompany their father part of the way to the sacred shrine in the grove and then halt as Oedipus enters to die.

CHORAL POEM

The Chorus sings a prayerful ode to the gods, asking them to let Oedipus die in peace and to enjoy a happy journey to the afterworld.

SCENE VIII, CHORAL DIALOGUE

Within moments, a messenger enters to announce that Oedipus is dead. The messenger says that Oedipus led Theseus and his daughters deep into the grove and said his farewell to them. He asked Theseus to care for his daughters after his death and then sent them away from him. Only Theseus accompanied Oedipus from that point on.

The messenger continues that as the two men walked along, Oedipus suddenly disappeared. Theseus was left alone, observing in wonder and awe the death of Oedipus. The messenger comforts the Chorus by saying that Oedipus obviously died without pain or agony. As the messenger concludes his story, Antigone and Ismene enter in mourning. They are frightened about what the future might hold for them now that their father is dead, but Theseus tells them that he will protect them always. Antigone asks to see her father's grave, but Theseus says the sacred location can't be revealed because Oedipus wished no one to disturb the quiet of his resting place. Antigone then decides to return with Ismene to Thebes, hoping to prevent the predicted deaths of her brothers on the battlefield. The Chorus concludes the play by saying, "Now let the weeping cease."

NOTE: In *Oedipus at Colonus* Sophocles reaches the zenith of his career, depicting with merciless clarity the decline and death of a great classical figure. The play recounts the original legend and puts to rest the troubled chronicle of Oedipus' children. There is much to recommend the play as an example of three-dimensional characterization and a tribute to the enduring and redeeming power of suffering. Oedipus achieves grandeur and dignity in this final play that deals with his life, and you are given a poignant sketch of a once-proud man who achieves wisdom in old age and peace in death.

ANTIGONE

The story of *Antigone* revolves around Oedipus' daughter, Antigone, and Creon, Oedipus' brother-in-law who has become king of Thebes. The opening of the story depicts in narrative a great battle that has just been fought. Although the city of Thebes has triumphed, it has lost its king in the fighting. Creon, the new king, decrees as his first official act that the body of Polyneices, the defeated invader, shall remain unburied as a symbol of corruption.

Creon's decree has barely been made public when he receives word that an attempt has been made to bury the corpse by the princess Antigone, sister of the dead Polyneices and niece of Creon. When Antigone is accused, she makes no attempt to conceal her deed and challenges Creon's right to make laws that are in conflict with the will of the gods, who have provided for religious burial and atonement for those killed in battle.

Creon, however, refuses to pardon Antigone for breaking his law. He sentences her to be walled up in a cave to die of suffocation. When Creon's son, Haimon, hears of the sentence to kill Antigone, he rushes to his father and begs him to spare her because she and he are engaged to be married. Creon refuses, and Haimon curses his father as he exits.

Next enters the wise, old prophet Teiresias. At first he urges Creon to reconsider the decrees concerning Polyneices and Antigone. Then he describes to Creon the frightful consequences that will befall him if he doesn't compromise his law. Creon is terrified. He has learned to believe Teiresias. He hurries out to supervise the burial of Polyneices and the release of Antigone. Too late. Antigone has hanged herself. With her is his son, who stabs himself as his father watches in horror. Returning to the palace with Haimon's body, Creon is greeted with the news that his wife, Eurydice, on hearing of her son's death, has also stabbed herself. Stunned and broken in spirit, Creon is led away as the play ends.

Antigone was a popular play and was frequently staged at the festival of Dionysus. Much of the play's success was due to the characterizations of Creon and Antigone, two of the most fully drawn character portraits of Sophocles. Creon, a pathetic man more patriotic and sincere than intentionally harmful, is a fine example of the authority figure who is too rigid and inflexible to admit mistakes or errors in judgment until it is too late. Antigone, a headstrong and passionate young woman more stubborn than sensible, is a fine example of the youthful and energetic crusader for right who refuses to compromise her principles, even when her life is threatened.

There are also many fine minor characters in the play, especially the dashing and handsome Haimon and the long-suffering Eurydice. The play itself has won critical acclaim as Sophocles' best poetic tragedy, especially in the writing of the choral odes. But the

popularity of the story is obviously due to its drama-
tization of human emotions and exploration of basic
principles of truth and justice.

PROLOGUE

The play begins as Antigone and Ismene, daughters of Oedipus, enter from the palace to discuss King
Creon's edict refusing burial to their brother, Polyneices, because he is considered a traitor to Thebes.
Antigone begs her sister to help bury Polyneices as an
act of conscience, but Ismene is afraid and refuses.
The sisters depart after Antigone ridicules Ismene's
weakness and timid assistance.

PARADOS

The Chorus enters to sing an ode of praise that
peace has been restored to the city with the recent
victory of the Theban army. It also describes the
bloody battle, particularly the combat in which the
brothers Eteocles and Polyneices killed each other in
hand-to-hand combat.

SCENE I

Creon, the new king of Thebes, enters to thank the
Chorus for its faith and loyalty. He promises to be a
wise ruler and pledges to keep the interests of the city
and its people foremost in his decisions. As the Chorus applauds Creon's wisdom, the king informs them
that Polyneices will not be buried because he is a "traitor." Creon hopes that the sight of Polyneices' decay-
ing body at the gates of the city will be an object lesson
to others. Creon is interrupted by a frightened sentry,
who reports that someone has attempted to bury Polyneices. Creon accuses the sentry of having accepted
a bribe to permit this to happen and threatens to exe-
cute him if the rebel is not found immediately.

ODE I

The Chorus chants a melodious ode proclaiming the beauty of nature and the wisdom of mankind. It concludes its song with an unexpected note of sadness as all are reminded that death visits even the greatest of men.

SCENE II

The sentry enters quickly with Antigone, who has been caught at the graveside of Polyneices. Antigone admits that she knew of Creon's edict but refused to obey it because it did not come from "God." Creon at first can't believe that his own niece would be the rebel who tried to bury the traitor Polyneices. He sends for Ismene to see what role she might have played in this treasonable act. Ismene tearfully confesses that she was a partner in the crime, but Antigone denies any help and insists that she acted alone. Creon decides that they are both insane and orders them taken away.

ODE II

The Chorus sings a sad ode that recalls the tragic story of the ancient curse that afflicted the descendants of the house of Labdacus—including Laios, Oedipus, and now the children of Oedipus. The Chorus points out that the laws of Zeus are divine and that no one can oppose the will of the gods.

SCENE III

Creon's son, Haimon, rushes in to plead for a pardon for Antigone. He tells his father that the citizens of Thebes are disturbed that she should suffer more, and he begs for mercy. Creon, however, refuses to

consider a pardon, and the two exchange bitter
words. Finally, Haimon furiously dismisses Creon
and rushes out. Creon suddenly compromises and
decides to spare the life of Ismene, but still refuses to
pardon Antigone. He decrees that Antigone must be
sealed in a cave outside the city walls and left to
die.

ODE III, SCENE IV

In a moving ode the Chorus praises the power of
love, and the goddess Aphrodite is hailed to work her
will on all those involved in this tragic scene. Antigone is brought in by the guards, and the Chorus is
saddened by her pitiful look. But Antigone will not
ask for mercy from Creon, and she refuses to humble
herself for violating Creon's edict. Instead, Antigone
chants her own ode and prepares to embrace her
grave as a "bridal bed," an everlasting prison in which
she will be condemned to a solitary death. Creon
enters and orders the guards to carry out his sentence.
Antigone is led away to the cave.

ODE IV

As the guards lead Antigone away, the Chorus
chants a melancholy song about well-known, defiant
figures of the past who have been subject to cruel and
harsh punishment for their beliefs. Antigone is included in the ode as one on whom "deathless fate"
laid a hard hand.

SCENE V

The blind prophet Teiresias now enters to warn
Creon that the gods are offended by his treatment of
Polyneices and will avenge themselves on the city.
Creon uncharacteristically refuses to heed the warn-
ings of the holy prophet, and Teiresias predicts that
the gods will show their displeasure by taking the life

of Haimon. Frightened by this horrible prediction, Creon appeals to the Chorus for guidance and then rushes out to give Polyneices a religious burial and to free Antigone from certain death.

PAEAN

The final ode of the Chorus is a joyful song of praise dedicated to the gods for giving Creon the wisdom to see the errors of his rash judgment.

EXODUS

Amid an air of celebration and rejoicing, a messenger enters to inform the audience that Haimon has killed himself after a bitter argument with his father. Antigone is also dead, having hanged herself. Eurydice, hearing the news of her son's death, also killed herself. Meanwhile, Creon returns carrying Haimon's body in his arms. He is overcome with remorse and sorrow and he begs the Chorus to lead him away. As he exits, Creon accepts responsibility for all the tragic events of the play and prays for his own death. The Chorus concludes the action by stating the moral of the play:

> There is no happiness where there is no wisdom;
> No wisdom but in submission to the gods.
> Big words are always punished,
> And proud men in old age learn to be wise.

NOTE: In *Antigone* Sophocles examined the characters of Creon and Antigone as human beings caught up in an age-old conflict—between following human laws and following divine laws. Antigone chooses to believe that divine laws are more important than man-made laws, and she willingly accepts her own death to prove the respect she has for religious duty. Creon, on the other hand, chooses to believe that man-made laws are more important than religious ideals. As a consequence of both their beliefs, the characters reflect noble and worthy principles of self-sacrifice and dedication to individual, personal laws of conduct.

Although the play is entitled *Antigone*, many critics consider Creon to be the tragic figure of a man who holds firmly to what he believes in, even though it costs him his son and his wife. Antigone, even though she suffers and dies, remains basically unchanged throughout the play and is never given an opportunity to express her warm and gentle spirit with either her sister Ismene or her fiancée Haimon. In spite of these apparent flaws, however, the character of Antigone is one of the most popular performance roles in theater history.

A STEP BEYOND

Tests and Answers

TESTS

Test 1

1. Sophocles does not explain Oedipus' past in _____
   his plays because
   A. his audience already knew it
   B. he starts in the middle to confuse the
      audience
   C. Oedipus should strike you as a man of
      mystery

2. The Chorus stands for _____
   A. the conscience of the community
   B. the common mob
   C. the audience's reactions

3. An antistrophe is _____
   A. the letdown after the climax
   B. a character who contrasts to the main
      character
   C. a verse in the Chorus' chants

4. At the beginning of *Oedipus the King*, _____
   Oedipus appears to be
   A. a harsh but effective tyrant
   B. a popular ruler, concerned for his people
   C. a king who has let his kingdom slide
      toward destruction

5. The oracles are at _____
   A. Cornith
   B. Colonus
   C. Delphi

6. Oedipus was asked to be king of Thebes   _____
   because
   A. he killed King Laios
   B. he married Queen Iocaste
   C. he solved the riddle of the Sphinx

7. Teiresias acts as   _____
      I. a fortune-teller
     II. a spokesman for the gods
    III. a trusted adviser
     IV. a holy man
   A. I and III only
   B. I, II, and IV only   C. II and III only

8. Oedipus suspects that he is being plotted   _____
   against by
   A. Creon and Teiresias
   B. the gods
   C. his wife Iocaste and their sons

9. Oedipus left his childhood home in Corinth   _____
   because
   A. he murdered a traveler at the crossroads
   B. he solved the riddle of the Sphinx
   C. he was afraid he would kill Polybos and
      marry Merope

10. Oedipus is punished by the gods because   _____
       I. he denied the truth of oracles
      II. he was a bad king
     III. he showed pride
    A. I, II, and III
    B. I and III only   C. II and III only

11. Discuss the skill with which Sophocles builds suspense
    and intrigue throughout his plays.

12. Discuss Sophocles' numerous references to sight as a
    symbol of seeing and knowing the truth.

13. Compare and contrast Oedipus and Creon as potential tragic heroes.

14. Discuss the role of the two messengers in *Oedipus the King*.

15. Interpret the following lines of dialogue by the Chorus as the final moral statement of *Oedipus the King*:

Let every man in mankind's frailty
Consider his last day; and let none
Presume on his good fortune until he find
Life, at his death, a memory without pain.

Test 2

1. Sophocles warned Athens of its imminent _____
   downfall in his plays because
   A. corruption and tyranny were rampant
   B. he felt shut out of the political life there
   C. the city was at its peak of power

2. In the Golden Age of Greece, drama was _____
   expected to
   A. help people forget their troubles
   B. teach a moral lesson
   C. surprise the audience with a suspenseful plot

3. The action of each of the Oedipus plays is _____
   supposed to take place over
   A. 2 hours
   B. 24 hours
   C. Oedipus' lifetime

4. There is a plague in Thebes because _____
   A. the gods are angry
   B. Oedipus has been neglecting his subjects
   C. the city is full of sin

5. The riddle of the Sphinx was, "Who moves   _____
   on four in the morning, on two at noon,
   and on three in the evening?" The answer is
   A. the sun
   B. Zeus
   C. man

6. The prophecy that has always hung over   _____
   Oedipus states that he will
   A. have no children
   B. kill his father and marry his mother
   C. lose his kingdom because a murder is
      unavenged

7. A good example of dramatic irony in   _____
   Oedipus the King is when
   A. Creon is reluctant to reveal the oracles'
      messages
   B. Oedipus vows to avenge Laios' murder
   C. Teiresias says Oedipus is the "pollution"
      of Thebes

8. Oedipus finally accepts the truth about   _____
   Laios' murderer when he hears it from
   A. Creon
   B. Teiresias
   C. a shepherd

9. When Oedipus learns Polybos has died, he   _____
   feels
      I. relieved, because the prophecy that
        he'll kill his father isn't true
     II. sad, because he loved Polybos
    III. glad, because now he will be king of
        Corinth as well as Thebes
   A. I and II only   B. II only
   C. I, II, and III

10. Physical blindness in these plays is a sign of _____
    A. ignorance
    B. moral wisdom
    C. favor with the gods

11. Trace the action of one of the plays by commenting on the structure of the episodes.

12. Sketch character portraits of Iocaste, Teiresias, and the shepherd. Discuss their roles, and comment on their relationships to Oedipus.

13. Discuss the purpose of Oedipus' blinding himself and its relationship to the theme of *Oedipus the King*.

14. Discuss the role of the Chorus. Cite specific examples of its "ideal spectator" function in commenting on the action.

15. Discuss Sophocles' use of the legend of Oedipus to express the theme, "man's fate determines his destiny."

ANSWERS

Test 1

1. A **2.** A **3.** C **4.** B **5.** C **6.** C

7. B **8.** A **9.** C **10.** B

    11. First show how Sophocles tells the Oedipus legend, beginning in the middle and withholding important facts until crucial moments in the play. Discuss how certain characters help to build suspense: Teiresias, Iocaste, the shepherd, and the messengers. Finally, select one scene to analyze more closely. Choose a moment when Oedipus receives a clue that his birth prophecy may indeed have come true; discuss what he knows and does not know at this point, and the dramatic irony felt by the audience.

12. Review the speeches of Teiresias and Oedipus; they will yield useful references for answering this question. You can discuss the imagery of sight in relation to the action of the plays, showing how the imagery changes as the plays progress, and pointing out how references to sight often come before major decisions are made by the characters. You can also discuss how the imagery relates to the characters. Compare how various characters define "blindness" and "vision," and explain how this helps you understand who they are. Finally, you can discuss how this imagery relates to the themes of the plays.

13. First define what a tragic hero is (see the Other Elements section of this guide). Then discuss how each of these two men fits that definition. Look especially at their speeches in Scene II and in the Exodus of *Oedipus the King*. Discuss how each is changed during the course of the play, and define what each one's tragic flaw might be.

In your final paragraph compare the two characters. Which is the better ruler for Thebes? Which is wiser? What are their relative strengths and weaknesses?

14. First discuss the structural use of the messengers to bring on news and heighten dramatic tension. (It may be useful to discuss here the problems created by the dramatic unities; refer to the Other Elements section.) How did this assist Sophocles in weaving together the present and past of the Oedipus legend? Discuss why Sophocles had to break Greek theatrical custom by using two messengers; compare them and the messages they bring. Next discuss how they function as dramatic figures; are their long monologues effective, and, if so, why? Finally, discuss how they relate to themes of the plays, especially to the themes of fate and the reversal of Oedipus' fortune.

15. First briefly define the moral statement that is being made by this passage. What does it mean to the characters? To the audience? Then go back through the play to show earlier statements of this same theme, especially by the Chorus. Discuss how this statement relates to the events you have seen in the play. End your answer with a detailed discussion of this speech, focusing on such phrases as "mankind's frailty," "presume on his good fortune," and "memory without pain." What are the meanings of this speech for Oedipus, and what are its meanings for you?

Test 2

1. C   2. B   3. B   4. A   5. C   6. B

7. B   8. C   9. A   10 B

11. In answering this question focus on the divisions of the play. (How are these divisions apparent in your text?) Pinpoint where the action of the play begins, in relation to the original legend. Then go through each of these sections: the Prologue; the Parados; each of the alternating scenes and choral odes; and the Exodus. Show how each one fits into the dramatic rhythms of the play, and explain what action takes place in it. Discuss in detail where the climax of the play comes, and how the action of the play is resolved.

12. Devote a paragraph to each of these characters. Briefly summarize who they are and what they might look like. Discuss their relationships with Oedipus and their attitudes toward him. What is each character's basic objective in the play? Then in a final paragraph compare the three characters. How are their actions similar? In what ways are they different?

13. Refer to Oedipus' dialogue with Teiresias in Scene I of *Oedipus the King* to define what blindness means at the beginning of the play. Then compare this to Oedipus' dialogue in the Exodus to show what blindness has taught Oedipus. Discuss Oedipus' blinding himself as an action: What do other characters, such as Creon and the Chorus, think of it? What does Oedipus himself feel he has accom-

plished with this act? Then discuss how Oedipus' blinding resolves the blindness imagery that has run through the play. Show how that imagery develops, how it relates to major themes, and what Oedipus' climactic blindness means thematically.

14. First discuss the traditional use of the Chorus in Greek drama. How did Sophocles change that in *Oedipus the King*, and to what effect? Next look at the sections where the Chorus appears alone, such as the Parados, Exodus, and stasima. What is the effect of these scenes? What function does the Chorus fulfill at these moments? Finally look at how the Chorus behaves in scenes with other characters. How do they interact with Oedipus, and why is this important? What is the effect of their speeches in these scenes? End with a definition of the "ideal spectator," and explain how it fits—or doesn't fit—the Chorus.

15. First state what the Athenian audience would already have known about Oedipus before the plays began. Then select three specific moments where the legend of Oedipus is used to advance the plot. How is information, which was standard from the legend, introduced into the action at each of these points? What is the effect of this information on Oedipus? How does this move ahead the action of the plot?

Finally discuss why Sophocles chose this legend to express his moral message. Do you think Oedipus' fate determines his destiny in the original legend? If so, show how Sophocles highlighted that in his plays. If you think this theme wasn't contained in the original legend, show how Sophocles added it in his dramatic treatment.

Term Paper Topics

Here are some suggested topics to help you develop critical and creative essays. When you write your essay, make sure you refer to specific dialogue or character actions that support your interpretation. Also try to give examples and references from the beginning, the middle, and the end of the play to suggest the continuity of the theme you're developing.

1. Discuss the role of the choral odes.

2. Discuss three examples of "warnings" Oedipus receives before he discovers the truth.

3. Defend Teiresias' initial refusal to identify Oedipus as the murderer of Laios.

4. Discuss the role of the messengers in providing information needed to develop the plot.

5. Trace the use of eye imagery in the dialogue of Teiresias and Oedipus.

6. Discuss the role that irony plays in revealing the truth about Oedipus.

7. Compare and contrast the two messengers and their roles.

8. Discuss *Oedipus the King* as a modern "murder-mystery."

9. Discuss the plays as lessons in inevitable human destiny.

10. Discuss Oedipus as a "tyrant figure."

11. Discuss the religious conflict between Oedipus and Teiresias.

12. Write a character sketch of Iocaste that shows her changing attitude toward Oedipus.

13. Discuss the political conflict between Oedipus and Creon.

14. Discuss the wisdom Oedipus gains through his suffering.

15. Trace the changing views of the Chorus from the beginning of a play to the end.

16. In what ways do Sophocles' plays reflect Greek religious views and beliefs?

17. What moral or religious lesson can the plays teach us today?

18. Discuss Sophocles' use of Ismene and Antigone to arouse pity for Oedipus.

19. Compare Oedipus and Creon—their values and their limitations.

20. What is the role of prophecy in developing the theme of fate?

21. Discuss Oedipus' confession of forgiveness in the Exodus of *Oedipus the King*.

22. Discuss the moral of the first play given by the Chorus in the Exodus.

23. Discuss Sophocles' use of the Oedipus legend in developing the plot.

24. What is Oedipus' tragic flaw?

25. What is the price Oedipus pays for self-knowledge?

26. Oedipus is sometimes seen as a Christ figure, sacrificing himself for the good of Thebes. Develop this theme using three examples.

27. Discuss the trilogy as plays about the relationship of man to the gods.

28. Compare and contrast Creon and Teiresias as noble spokesmen for the truth.

29. Discuss Oedipus' self-righteousness in his scenes with Creon and Teiresias.

30. Discuss the role of justice by citing three examples.

31. Compare and contrast Creon's and Oedipus' decisions to exile themselves from Thebes.

32. Discuss the atmosphere of "impending doom" that hangs over *Oedipus the King*.

33. Discuss Oedipus' excessive pride, or hubris.

34. Discuss the plays as a commentary of moral corruption.

35. Compare and contrast Iocaste's roles as queen, mother, and wife.

36. Write a character sketch of the Chorus as an "ideal spectator."

37. Discuss the implications of Creon's becoming king of Thebes.

Glossary

Acropolis Elevated and walled section of Athens where the festival of Dionysus was held.

Antistrophe The second of three parts in the Greek choral ode. It is delivered as the Chorus circles back toward the orchestra, moving from left to right.

Apollo The god of prophecy, reward, and punishment. Apollo was the son of Zeus and the most respected of the Greek gods.

Artemis The twin sister of Apollo and the goddess of the heavens. Artemis was known to send plagues and sudden deaths—especially to women—without warning.

Athene The goddess of power and wisdom. Athene was known as the protector of the Athenian state and was responsible for maintaining Greek law and order.

Cithaeron A mountain range that separated the province of Boeotia, where Thebes was located, from the surrounding frontier of Attica. Cithaeron was thought to be sacred to Dionysus.

Colonus City near Athens where Oedipus dies.

Delphi The most sacred city in Greece, home of the holy oracles of Apollo.

Dionysus God of wine and fertility; proprietor of the theater.

Exodus A choral recessional in Greek tragedy. It is the ritual departure song of the Chorus as it moves off the stage at the end of the play.

Furies The Eumenides, or "gracious ones," who punished people for disobedience.

Hubris Excessive pride.

Oracles Priests or psychics believed to be in direct communication with the gods. The Greeks believed oracles were holy prophets, capable of predicting the future and also interpreting the past and the present. The most famous oracle was located at Delphi.

Parados The ceremonial entrance of the Chorus; it is also the first song chanted by the Chorus as it enters the theater and moves to the orchestra.

Prologue Literally, "the speech before." In Greek tragedy the prologue is the first passage of spoken dialogue before the entrance of the Chorus.

Sphinx A winged monster known in myth as "the strangler." The Sphinx had a lion's body and the head and breasts of a woman. Sitting on a rock outside the gates of Thebes, the Sphinx asked the same riddle of every passerby. Those who could not answer the riddle were strangled. When Oedipus solved the riddle of the Sphinx, she flung herself from the rock and was killed.

Stasimon The choral song chanted or sung by the Chorus in its ritual movement around the stage. Stasima alternate with passages of spoken dialogue and are also found as choral odes between individual episodes of the tragedy.

Strophe The first of three parts of the Greek choral ode. It is delivered as the Chorus circles from right to left in the orchestra; it comes before the antistrophe.

Thebes The chief city of the province of Boeotia, reportedly founded by the hero Cadmus. Legend had it that Thebes was created when Amphion played his magic lyre and caused stones and rocks to move into place to form a city. Oedipus is a descendant of Cadmus.

Zeus The husband of Hera, Zeus was the most powerful of all the Greek gods and was entrusted with ruling Mount Olympus.

Further Reading

CRITICAL WORKS

Adams, Sinclair. *Sophocles the Playwright*. Toronto: University of Toronto Press, 1957.

Arnott, Peter. *An Introduction to the Greek Theatre*. New York: St. Martin's, 1958.

Bowra, C.M. *Sophoclean Tragedy*. Oxford: Clarendon Press, 1944.

Fergusson, Francis. "Oedipus: The Tragic Rhythm of Action." In *The Idea of a Theatre*. Princeton: Princeton University Press, 1968, pp. 13–41.

Kirkwood, G.M. *A Study of Sophoclean Drama*. Ithaca: Cornell University Press, 1958.

Kitto, H.D.F. *Greek Tragedy*. Garden City: Anchor Press, 1954.

Norwood, Gilbert. *Greek Tragedy*. Ithaca: Cornell University Press, 1928.

Schroeter, James. "The Four Fathers: Symbolism in Oedipus." In *Criticism*, III (Summer, 1961): 185–200.

Waldock, A.J. *Sophocles the Dramatist*. Cambridge: Cambridge University Press, 1951.

Webster, T.B.L. *Introduction to Sophocles*. Oxford: Oxford University Press, 1936.

Whitman, C.H. *Sophocles*. Cambridge: Harvard University Press, 1951.

Woodard, Thomas. *Sophocles: A Collection of Critical Essays*. Englewood Cliffs, N.J.: Prentice-Hall, 1966.

AUTHOR'S WORKS

Sophocles wrote more than 100 plays. The following seven have survived; the approximate year each was written is given in parentheses.

Ajax (445 B.C.)
Antigone (442 B.C.)
Oedipus the King (425 B.C.)
Philoctetes (409 B.C.)
Electra (408 B.C.)
Trachiniae (408 B.C.)
Oedipus at Colonus (407 B.C.)

The Critics

Here are some thought-provoking and stimulating comments from major critics who have studied the Oedipus trilogy. These brief excerpts should help you with an overall view of the plays and the characters and may give you ideas for further reading or research when writing your papers or essays.

A perfect tragedy should imitate actions which excite pity and fear, and also effect the proper purgation of these emotions. The change of fortune presented should be that of a man who is not eminently good and just, yet whose misfortune is brought about not by vice or depravity, but by some error or frailty. He must be one who is highly renowned and prosperous—a personage like Oedipus, or other illustrious men of such families. The plot ought to be so constructed that, even without the aid of the eye, he who hears the tale told will thrill with horror and melt with pity at what takes place. This is the impression we should receive from hearing the story of Oedipus.
—Aristotle, *The Poetics*

Oedipus is man rather than an individual tragic hero. The play is characteristic of the Greek attitude towards men to see him not only as an individual but also as an individual in society, a political being as well as a private person.
—Bernard Knox, *Oedipus at Thebes*, 1957

The basic conflict in the play is most simply defined as one between man and god: The king's belief in reason and doing one's duty is smashed by a mysterious, immovable, supernatural force.
—Gilbert Norwood, *Greek Tragedy*, 1928

The gods of Sophocles are not like the God we are used to hearing about in the *Bible*. Our God rules absolutely, giving mercy and making judgment. The classical gods do not judge, they are merely forces of right or wrong. Judgment is the work of *fate*, and means simply to give a man his due.

—Tom Driver, *Oedipus the King*, 1961

. . . the proud tragic view of Sophocles sees in the fragility and inevitable defeat of human greatness the possibility of a purely human heroism to which the gods can never attain, for the condition of their existence is everlasting victory.

—Bernard Knox, *Oedipus at Thebes*, 1957

Each single incident in the play is the sort of thing that can and does happen. Sophocles does not blame these people; neither therefore must we; it is not a matter of guilt and punishment, but of how people can in fact be deceived.

—H.D.F. Kitto, *Greek Tragedy*, 1954

Oedipus' . . . humiliation is a lesson both to others and to him. Democritus' words, "the foolish learn modesty in misfortune," may be applied to Oedipus, who has indeed been foolish in his mistakes and illusions and has been taught modesty through suffering.

—C.M. Bowra, *Sophoclean Tragedy*, 1944

Sophocles' chorus is a character that takes an important role in the action of the play. The chorus may be described as a group personality, like an old Parliament. It has its own traditions, habits of thought and feeling.

—Francis Fergusson, *The Idea of a Theatre*, 1968

Sophocles plays continually on the opposition of light and darkness, sight and blindness. In the Teiresias scene, Oedipus is revealed as mentally blind to his real position and the dangers which surround him. It is the blind prophet who has true knowledge. At the end of the play, when Oedipus has found the truth, he destroys the sense organs which had led him into error. He is now blind, but sees truly.

—Peter Arnott, *Oedipus the King*, 1960